Beyond
the Laughter...

Beyond the Laughter...

A Daughter's Story of Curly's Post Three Stooges Years

Grace Garland

Writers Club Press
San Jose   New York   Lincoln   Shanghai

Beyond the Laughter...
A Daughter's Story of Curly's Post Three Stooges Years

Writers Club Press
an imprint of iUniverse, Inc.

For information address:
iUniverse, Inc.
5220 S. 16th St., Suite 200
Lincoln, NE 68512
www.iuniverse.com

ISBN: 0-595-20846-0

Printed in the United States of America

PROLOGUE

When I was first approached about writing this book I was somewhat skeptical of the validity of this woman who claimed to be the daughter of Curly of the famous Three Stooges. I agreed to meet with her and listen to her story.

As a courtesy and out of curiosity I planned a stop to her hometown on my way to another destination. When I saw her I knew she was whom she claimed to be, except for her long hair, she looked just like him!

As I listened to her story I found myself so enthralled, it was as if I was under a spell! The story was so amazing I just had to hear more. Like most people, I had always thought of Curly as the moronic stooge rather than a 'family' man! Needless to say I canceled my other plans.

It took a year to gather the information needed to write her story and to verify certain aspects of it.

Getting to know her I realized there was no way she could have invented this story. In researching the events and people she spoke about, I found her story to be amazingly accurate. As a teacher, I was aware of the struggles she had faced trying to gain access to the material she needed to go forward with this book due to her lack of formal education. Material her father had said, "Will be your proof of who you are, and who your father was." Her education had been interrupted by her mother in an effort to protect her from Curly's unsavory 'family' business and their associates.

I developed a deep respect and affection for this woman named Jacqueline, and I hope through the publication of this book she will gain closure and grant her father's final request and "Go beyond the laughter".

CHAPTER ONE

Irene Scott had long, dark chestnut hair, green eyes, and a body that disguised her mere thirteen years.

She had three older siblings. Twenty–one year old Marie, had married at age fourteen and moved to Georgia. She visited as often as possible and wrote faithfully. Irene was ten years younger than her twin brothers, Cal and Gus. To look at them, you'd never know they were twins. Cal was tall and thin, with light brown hair, hazel eyes camouflaged by thick distorting lenses encased in black rims. Gus, on the other hand, was short and stocky, with dark brown hair and hazel eyes. He had thick, bushy eyebrows that grew across the bridge of his nose. Irene teased her big brothers calling them 'Mutt and Jeff'.

Cal was the first born by six minutes, was always the leader, Gus, the follower. Neither were angels, both drank hard liquor and smoked cigarettes; Cal smoked Raleigh, Gus preferred Lucky Strike.

Cal spent time behind bars as a juvenile for shoplifting and defacing school property. Gus usually tagged along with Cal on these excursions, but somehow Cal always knew how to defend him or shove him under something out of the way of authorities. Therefore, Cal spent more time in jail than Gus who didn't have quite as sharp an edge as Cal.

While in jail, Cal had not been as tough as on the outside, and after a prison gang bang at the age of nineteen, discovered he preferred men to women. Although Cal was a homosexual, nobody on the outside would have dared mentioned it aloud, and no one would have lived through having called him 'queer' or any other word demeaning his manhood.

As he grew older, Gus was a thief as well, but little girls rather than other men whetted his sexual appetite.

When not in jail, Cal did odd jobs on the Tampa shrimp boats, was a member of the Klu Klux Klan, and when called upon did work for the notorious Trafficante mafia 'family'.

Gus had a legitimate job as cook on a shrimp boat, the Tampa Queen.

Once after several days on the shrimp boat, Gus stopped in at his favorite bar, the Saratoga, to unwind. There he met a man he recognized as a celebrity. Gus bought him a couple of drinks and they became fast drinking buddies. Gus remembered it was his little sister's birthday and convinced his new pal to go home with him as a gift for Irene.

Upon arriving, Irene said, "Hey, I know you! You're a Stooge!" Gus began to laugh, "Oh yeah, I don't even know your real name." The Stooge smiled at Irene, "Curly...you can just call me Curly." Irene was star struck! All afternoon she had him making his famous 'N'yuk, N'yuk, N'yuk and 'whoop, whoop' sounds, as well as, curling his lip. He even showed her how to do some of the Stooge stunts like poking the eyes and bopping the head using Gus as the straight man. At one point, Irene asked Curly to show her how to curl her lip. As they sat on the couch he demonstrated for her, then she tried it, but couldn't master it. He moved closer to her and took his hand to place her lip in the correct position. She couldn't hold the position; they both got tickled and laughed so hard they slid off the couch into the floor. Irene landed smack on top of him! He quickly helped her back on the couch, where they continued laughing. Then Irene announced to him that she was an artist as well, and read some of her poems and sang one of the songs she had written. "Do you want to hear my favorite song I have written?" she asked enthusiastically. "Sure. Go ahead. Sing it for me." She breathed deeply, "Ok, here goes. Now remember I don't write the music down on paper, I just know it in my head. I can't write music, yet.

I woke up screaming your name late last night
I had a bad dream that we had a fight.

You said that you didn't love me anymore
I watched helplessly as you walked out the door."

"I'm going to be famous one day, too." She announced with certainty. He replied, "If you keep that up you'll be more famous than I ever dreamed of! I'll tell you what, when you're a little older I'll try to help you get your music to the right people." She smiled and dropped her head coyly.

Irene's mother began to take notice as the clowning became more flirtatious. She was ready to end the party and had Irene's father, also a cook on a shrimp boat, cut the cake he had made her in a small–galvanized washtub!

This would become the most memorable birthday Irene would ever have, as it was the birthday she met the man who in time would become her one true love.

Irene never got Curly out of her mind. Frequently Gus would run into him in Tampa, and if Cal were not around he would take Curly home with him. Curly was born maternally into the Patrillo family, a rival 'family' of Trafficante, whose long arm reached from Georgia to the West Coast. Therefore, it was not a good idea for Cal and Curly to be associated. The rivalry between families would cause too much tension between the two.

Curly tried to do as little of his 'family' business as possible. He wanted a different kind of life, but could never turn his back on his 'family', and at times their wants and needs superceded his own.

Curly's Mother was the daughter of the Patrillo family 'Don'. His father had nothing to do with his wife's family business; the Don referred to him as his daughter's 'pet', and allowed her to keep him as long as he behaved. He unsuccessfully tried to shield Curly from the Patrillo 'family' influence.

Irene was completely unaware of Cal or Curly's underworld affiliations; she just knew she wanted to be near Curly. For nearly four years Irene dreamed of the time she could say aloud to Curly her innermost feelings.

She knew in her heart he felt the same, because when her father died he came by to express his condolences. She walked him to the car, and before she knew what was happening, she was in his arms. She knew by his touch this was not 'fatherly' concern, that he like her, wanted more.

A few days later she overheard Gus and Curly planning a trip west. Curly had to go to California to fulfill studio commitments, and he wanted to hire Gus as a cook on his yacht. Irene seized the opportunity to be near Curly. She made her plans to stow away on the yacht. She wanted to pursue her two dreams, Curly and her song writing. After all, he had promised to help her when she was older, she could think of no better time than the present!

When Curly left, Irene quickly wrote down the name of the yacht, the 'Carabella' at pier number nine. She planned carefully to get to the boat just prior to their arrival so she wouldn't be missed at home, and would not be seen by Curly or Gus, until they were well at sea.

At 5:30p.m. While there was still light, Irene crept up the pier and onto the 'Carabella', she located the safety boats and crawled inside pulling the tarp that covered the dingy, over her. She had packed a bologna sandwich, a thermos of iced tea, and two Oreo cookies. She planned to make her presence known at breakfast. She found it hard to sleep so she slipped out of the dingy when she thought everyone was asleep. It had been raining and the wind was blowing too much for her to enjoy the ride on deck. She crawled back into the dingy covering herself with the tarp. She played the scenes over and over in her mind about making her grand entrance, until she fell asleep.

The morning light shown on the tarp and the heat became almost unbearable. Irene awoke with a start! She got her bearings and slowly slipped out of the dingy. As she breathed the fresh ocean air, a breeze carrying the smell of bacon drifted up from the kitchen. Irene loved Gus's cooking almost as much as she had her father's. This morning it would be especially good.

She waited a few minutes, rehearsing her entrance, adjusting her clothes and combing her hair with the comb she had tucked into her bra. The smell of breakfast was getting more and more tempting. She began walking slowly toward the delicious aroma. She smelled coffee, and just as she started to open the door, she heard unfamiliar voices on the other side! Suddenly she felt very sick in the pit of her stomach, "What if I have gotten on the wrong yacht?" she whispered. Putting her ear to the door, she continued listening, hoping to hear Curly or Gus. Finally, she heard Gus's familiar voice asking if anyone needed more coffee. She breathed a sigh of relief and placed her trembling hand on the doorknob, opening it slowly. There sat Curly dressed in a captain's outfit, and two men she didn't recognize in dark suits. The look on Curly's face let her know she had nothing to fear. He stood up, took her hand and seated her beside him. Gus snapped, "How the hell…" Curly interrupted, "Gus, bring our guest some breakfast, please." Gus was shocked that Irene had the gumption to do what she had done. Later he made sure she had left their mother a note explaining herself. Irene assured him she had. She didn't confide in Gus her feelings for Curly, and she knew that Curly had not brought the subject up with him either. She knew how Curly felt, but she was also aware that because of their more than twenty–five year age difference, they had to be discreet and take their relationship slowly.

Curly gave Irene the main cabin and he took the smaller one. He made sure she was well taken care of, he even gave her permission to choose an evening gown from the closet to wear to dinner, telling her his mother and sister were always prepared.

Curly excused himself from his guests that evening and invited Irene to dine with him on deck. The table was set with candlelight and Gus made her favorite, spaghetti. She had her first taste of what would become her drink of choice, Peach Schnapps. The music seemed to fill the air as Irene and Curly danced under the stars. Curly was a wonderful dancer and she found herself gliding across the deck as if they were Fred and Ginger! The darkness made the night magical! The water pounded the side of the yacht sprinkling a fine mist through the night air. The sky was bursting with stars appearing to skip across the dark horizon. Although it was midsummer, the ocean breeze gave Irene a slight chill. Curly retrieved her wrap from the chair, came up behind her, gently draping it over her shoulders. They stood like this for several minutes, no words had to be spoken. Curly turned her to him and kissed her more passionately than she had ever imagined a kiss could be. Curly knew he could have taken advantage of this sweet young girl and the situation, but he knew he was falling in love and he wanted the woman that was to be his wife to be pure, even from him. Although he knew he would not allow himself to make love to her, he pressed her close so she could feel the hardness of his manhood. He wanted to caress her breasts, but requited the urge. Suddenly, he pushed her away and said, "We can't." She wiped her mouth with the back of her hand and dropped her head in flushed anguish and embarrassment. Curly pulled her to him, lifted her chin, gently kissed her cheek, took her hand, and led her to her cabin. He kissed her again at the door, this time more passionately than before. He could see the bed from the door and wanted to be in with her more at this moment than words could describe. This time it was Irene that pushed him away. He smiled as she closed the door. Sleep was erratic for both, and dreams were hot and wet.

They traveled for three weeks; the first two days Curly conducted his 'family' business while Gus gave Irene cooking lessons. The rest of the days were spent getting to know each other, playing cards, (he taught her to play poker), she sang her songs to him, and he told her about himself, (excluding his 'family' business).

Each night was more romantic than the first, but never culminating in copulation, as they agreed that Irene should remain a virgin until she married. They stopped at several points along the way for Curly to conduct his business; the first stop was New Orleans, where the two businessmen disembarked. Irene was never properly introduced to them. They were off the yacht before she knew anything about it; in fact, she never gave them a second thought after seeing them at the table that first morning.

New Orleans was Irene's favorite stop. She fell in love with French and Cajun foods. Curly took her to a few Jazz clubs where she found the music to be surprisingly wonderful! She hoped she would be able to return to New Orleans someday…with Curly.

Although California was a dream come true for Irene, she was unsure what lay in store for her once she arrived. Her relationship with Curly was well defined in the confines of the yacht, but she wasn't sure how it would be once they docked. She realized that she had made plans for this trip with her heart and not her head. She had thirty dollars to her name that she had saved babysitting. She kept a neighbor's baby after school, while its mother took care of an ill parent. Most of that went to help her mother with bills and groceries. Since her father's death, her mother had precious little money and Irene had to pitch in. Cal helped with the rent, (when he wasn't in jail), and Gus helped when he wasn't on the shrimp boats. She wished she had been able to plan better, but she didn't know she would be leaving so abruptly. She was unsure if she would stay in California or go back with Gus, if he were going back. 'I'll have to ask Gus to loan me some money until I get a job,' she thought, 'I'll pay him back somehow,' she promised herself.

Though Curly didn't discuss his business, Irene knew he must have obligations in his show business endeavors, she was afraid his attentions might turn to some buxom, blonde, bombshell and he would forget all about her. She knew she was really too young for this man she loved so much, and had not been able to get off her mind or out of her heart for the past four years. She allowed her mind to wonder about how Curly really felt. He was a man of few words, not at all in person as he appeared on screen. He was like a college textbook and she a kindergarten child, the words and meanings were there, the pictures were clear, but the child couldn't read the words or understand the meanings. She knew she had to stay pure, interested, and give him the space he needed no matter how hard it would be.

As the trip drew to an end, Irene prayed for the last night to be special. She wanted to be in his arms again, just one more time. To feel the love she knew he had for her, even though neither had ever professed it aloud, she knew it was true. She had to savor this one last night, as she had no idea what tomorrow would bring.

Gus cooked a steak dinner that last night. Unfortunately, the rain prevented eating on the deck, so they dined in Irene's cabin. The candles flickered across Curly's face as he spoke his plans for her. He told her he would introduce her to several friends that owned nightclubs. He would pull a few favors so she would be allowed to work in the bar even though she was under aged. She would need to keep her mouth shut about how old she was, "Ladies don't discuss their ages anyway, so if asked, say that," he advised. He said she may have to start as a hatcheck or cigarette girl, but he would try to see that someone took notice of her songs. He said he had an apartment he only used when he had clients in town on 'family' business, and she would stay there. She would be safe, he would see to it. He gave her two hundred dollars and told her that when they docked he would take her to the apartment.

The next day they docked, Curly paid Gus his wages and gave him his airplane ticket home. Gus told Irene goodbye and gave her fifty dollars in case of an emergency. She hugged him and told him to smooth things out with their mother for her. He smiled, kissed her on the forehead and whispered, "Is this what you really want?" Nodding, she smiled, hugged him and he left.

Curly kept his promise to Irene, found her a job as a cigarette girl at the famed Brown Derby. Irene made good money and great tips. She sent her mother money from her first paycheck with a letter telling her how happy she was and assuring her she was still a 'good' girl. She told her all the wonderful things Curly had seen to on her behalf. She gave her the address and asked her to write often.

After a few weeks, Irene saw very little of Curly. He was busy making public appearances as well as with 'family' business. The only promise Curly hadn't kept so far was the one he made about her music. She believed he would still make good on his word, so in her spare time she continued writing her songs.

Curly fulfilled his contract and was able to spend more time with Irene. She could hardly believe she had been in California two years!

One night after her shift Curly was waiting for her at the apartment. Tom Warren, a friend of his from the studio had told him of a party being held at a studio and Curly wanted her to be the cigarette girl for the party. He said it would not interfere with her job; it would be after her regular shift at the Derby. He told her not to bother coming home to change clothes, wear her uniform, and he would send a taxi for her.

Irene was excited about the party because he had told her many important people would be there. She was glad he was finally going to keep his last promise to her. She asked him who would be at the party and he said, "Hell, J. Edgar Hoover will probably be there, and who knows, at these things all kinds of giants show up. Wally Berry, Gable, Disney, big guns from all the lots, producers, people in the music industry, like Sinatra, and whatever politicians happen to be in town. The President has even been known to make an appearance! Generally these are quite impressive parties, many big deals have been made at parties like these." he said.

Irene could hardly wait for her shift at the Derby to end. She was excited and nervous! She followed Curly's instructions to the letter, leaving the Derby as soon as her shift ended; the taxi was waiting just as he had said it would be. Curly was waiting for her in front of the studio. He was smoking a cigar and pacing like an expectant father. As the taxi pulled to the curb Curly threw the cigar to the ground and opened the door. He paid the fare and as the taxi pulled away he kissed Irene on the cheek, "I'm glad to see you, Babe." On the way inside he gave her orders to sell the goods and remain silent otherwise. Once inside, the studio was crowded. Trying her best not to show it, Irene was amazed by the people she was seeing in person instead of on the movie screen! There were several beautiful girls mingling, she didn't recognize, she asked, "Who are they?" Curly replied, "Oh, the ones you don't recognize are the new breed, the starlets, looking for a break. Most of those girls would do anything to get a big break in show business, they're not your type, just don't get friendly with them." Many of the other stars she had seen at the Derby, but not this many at once! Curly had to tell her to be still twice while helping her to put the cigarette tray on! He chuckled at her childlike wonder, as he said, "Now don't get too star struck, Irene. Remember what I told you just sell the goods. How do you make it at the Derby? Haven't you ever seen a movie star besides me there?" "Not this many! Not all together!" she replied as she continued to stare at the crowd. "Well, don't ask any of them for their autograph!" he laughed. "Ha! Ha! You're funny, Mr. Stooge!" she jested as she made a face and stuck her tongue out at him. "And don't do that at anybody else, they would think you were doing it for other reasons!" he commanded. "Huh? What do you mean?" she asked naively. "Just don't be doing that to anybody, that's all." He said with his teeth clenched. He took her hand and pointed to the place he wanted her to begin. "Oh, I brought my songs just in case." She took his hand and pulled him to where he had stashed her purse, with all the other coats and purses. She handed him several pages folded this way and that, without a word, he stuffed them in his coat pocket. Then, like an obedient child, she did as she was told.

"Cigars, cigarettes," she called with a smile, as she worked the crowd. She was making good tips and seemed to be pleasing Curly. Occasionally a movie star or other famous figure would ask her name, or comment about how pretty she was. After about two hours, someone popped her on the butt and tried to pull her into his lap. Everyone around was laughing and drinking, not caring what they were doing. Irene cared, as did Curly. He rushed over and grabbed her arm, pulling her away, "All right, Edgar, have a cigar, they're from Cuba." He accepted the cigar and said, "Is she yours Curly? She's mighty pretty! What's her name?" "You're good at solving puzzles Edgar, hell you probably knew it before I did!" they laughed, Curly took Irene's hand and they moved on. "Don't worry about Edgar, Baby, he didn't mean anything by what he did, you're not his type. You're too female." "Was that Mr. Hoover? What did you mean by what you just said?" "Never mind it was a joke, and not a very funny one." Curly slipped the tray from around her neck, took her hand and led her into a dressing room. They were alone, no talking, Curly took a drink while Irene watched. Then he reached behind a chair and took out a bottle of Peach Schnapps and a paper cup already brimming with the nectar. Irene began feeling the effects of what she assumed was the Schnapps and excitement almost immediately. As they headed back to the studio, Irene noticed the crowd had dwindled somewhat. Curly was shaking hands and speaking to almost everyone. He appeared to be very popular. Someone yelled at him from mid–air. Irene and Curly looked up to see one of the studio camera-men on a camera boom. He was turning around and around. Someone handed Irene another drink as someone else turned on the bright lights. Curly grabbed Irene and twirled her around as if she were a tiny ballerina in a child's jewelry box. Suddenly, someone took Curly's place and twirled her around even more. She began to feel dizzy, and the last thing she remembered was seeing Curly's face in the crowd as she was spun around.

The next afternoon Irene awoke in her apartment, still in uniform, but it was ripped at the waist and the halter strap was broken, a trench coat she did not recognize was draped over her. There was five hundred dollars, with a twenty being the smallest denomination, laying on the night table. As Irene forced herself out of bed, she couldn't understand why she was so sore. Her head ached, she dismissed that as retaliation from the Schnapps, but she couldn't account for the bruises and other marks on her body. She began shaking as she examined the rest of her battered body. Her thighs were blue with red streaks, and between her legs were nearly black. Her left breast had been bitten; the teeth marks were deep, black and blue, and swollen. There were fingerprints on both her wrists and a palm print on her right shoulder. The more she looked the more afraid she became. She felt violated, alone, and betrayed. She wanted Curly, she needed him to tell her she was all right and explain what had happened. She went to the phone and tried to call him. Her resources were limited, as he had given her just two numbers, his apartment and the bar he frequented most. He was at neither.

Irene got in the shower, turned the water on full blast, as hot as she could stand it. She wanted to cleanse herself of the unknown events that had taken place. The beating water made her bludgeoned skin feel like pins and needles pricking it. She stood under the water and screamed. When she finished the shower she curled up on the sofa in the dark to think about what she would say to Curly to find out what happened at the party. That was, if she ever saw him again. She had to know what happened, and she knew he had the answers. She called in sick at the Derby. This would be the first night she had not gone to work.

A few nights later Curly came to the apartment. He was quieter than usual. She was more nervous than she had anticipated; she was quite unsure how to approach the subject and was hoping he would. He didn't. Finally, Irene broke the silence, "Curly, what happened to me the other night at the party?" "Irene I'm sorry things got a little out of hand, but since you are alright, things are better left alone." "A little out of hand, I'm alright?" she snapped in a raised voice. "What do you mean? Look at the bruises on my legs and my wrists! How can you say I'm alright? How can you be so…so calm! Don't you care Curly?" "Of course I care! It's just that some things are better left the hell alone, Irene. You can't change what happened, I can't change what happened so damn it, forget it!" "You forget it! I can't! Did you do this to me, Curly?" "Hell no! I would never hurt you like that! How dare you accuse me of that!" "Oh, Curly I'm sorry. I didn't mean to accuse you. I just want to know what happened. If you didn't do it then who did?" "Please, Irene let it go, please. For my sake just leave it be! I love you isn't that enough?" "I love you too, and yes it is enough!" She wanted to know if she was still virginal, but somehow she just couldn't allow him to know she had her doubts. She was afraid he would loose his respect for her, and in turn she would loose him.

Curly told her he had to leave California. His family needed him to come home for awhile. His uncle was ill and his mother had sent for him. Irene was a little jealous of Curly being able to go home. It had been over two years since she had seen her family. She wanted to talk to her mother and make her understand how much she loved Curly and he loved her. She knew her concerns, but thought she could put her mind at ease. A few weeks after Curly left, Irene received word from her mother that Cal and Gus were in trouble and she needed to come home. Irene was sad that California had not proven to be the break she had hoped for, and Curly had promised her. Still, she was glad she had gotten to know Curly better and had established her independence.

She packed her bags, collected her pay, and for the first time in her life, flew in an airplane.

CHAPTER TWO

Irene went to court with her mother in support of her brothers. She had never been in a courtroom before and was visibly nervous.

The air in the courtroom was thick with uncertainty as the chairs began to fill with spectators. Cal and Gus were on trial for felonious assault of a young woman. It was hard for Irene to think about her brothers beating a woman. As she thought about it, the memories of her own battered and bruised body crept to the forefront of her mind. Unbeknown to her, the deed was an order for her brothers, and a warning to the young woman from one of the 'families'.

Irene looked beautiful in her black and white polka–dot dress with black and white spectator pumps. Her chestnut hair lay across her shoulders, beneath the picture hat framing her lovely face. Rebel red lipstick looked good with her olive complexion. Her naturally long, dark eyelashes curled when they touched her high cheekbones. She sat with one glove and her handbag on her lap looking straight ahead. The back of her neck was tingling as if someone were staring at her. She bowed her head demurely and cut her eyes across the aisle, it was Curly! It took all the restraint she had not to run to him. Seeing him took her breath away, she felt flush. Suddenly, there were sweat beads slowly dripping between her breasts. She wondered what he was thinking and how he was feeling being so close to her, yet so far away. He winked at her, her body became weak; her purse and glove fell out of her lap. The glove landed in the aisle. He retrieved it, put it to his lips and kissed it. She took a deep breath and looked toward the ceiling, the sound of the gavel banging caused her to jump slightly in her seat. A hush fell over the room and brought Irene back to the ugly business at hand.

The Judge pushed the sleeves of his black robe up to his elbows and leaned forward calling Cal and Gus to face him. He was ready to pronounce their sentence. Irene and her mother held hands so tightly their knuckles turned white. The Judge called them 'animals', saying had there been proof of molestation he would have seen to it they rotted under the jail! Irene had not been made aware her brothers had been in jail for over a year, and was somewhat relieved when the Judge suspended their guilty sentence to time served, and three years probation.

A tear balanced in the corner of Mrs. Scott's eye and she dabbed it away with the yellowed lace handkerchief she had carried on her wedding day. She wasn't superstitious, but she had brought the handkerchief thinking it couldn't hurt to have something at the trial that was reminiscent of a happier time.

The Judge continued to revile Cal and Gus regarding their animalistic deed and warned that should either of them appear before him again they would be old men before they saw the light of day!

As the gavel pounded in dismissal and the bailiff called, "All rise", Irene was glad to see the Judge step down and leave the room. She turned to smile at Curly, but to her disappointment he wasn't there. She surveyed the remaining spectators inside and out of the courtroom, still no Curly.

Once outside Cal and Gus joined them. Their mother was so glad to have her arms around her children once more; she didn't want to let them go. It was hard for her to admit her sons were 'animals', she wondered how she had let them down. Her guilt for their behavior kept her from scolding them, too much. She had tried to instill certain traits in them; they had not heeded her wise advice. Their father had been a hard worker, up before dawn and to bed before dark, when he was ashore. The only role he had played in their lives was that of provider. He was a good man, but it was all he could do to make a living. It had been that way for him growing up, and he knew no better way.

Cal and Gus were not evil really; they were just weak.

They had an insatiable appetite for things they couldn't afford, and the things the world said they shouldn't have. Neither could say no to their *unnatural* wants and needs.

A long black car with tented windows pulled up to the curb. The back window was rolled halfway down expelling cigar smoke; a voice called to Cal. Irene couldn't see the face the voice belonged to, but shortly after, Cal motioned for Gus to join them. Gus walked to the car as Cal got in. Gus closing the door, continued to speak through the opened window. The window began to roll up as Gus rejoined Irene and his mother. As usual, no questions were asked. Irene, Gus and their mother went home.

Irene was disappointed that Curly had disappeared from the courtroom, and as usual, she couldn't get him off her mind. She went to her room to change clothes. As she slipped out of her dress, she seemed to lose herself in thought. The windows were raised and the fan oscillated, breezing her body occasionally. The thought of Curly again made her body burn for his touch. She closed her eyes and allowed her fingertips to gently trace her cheek and neck as he had done so many times before. The spell was broken when her mother called to her, "Irene, come make lunch." Irene quickly dressed in her blue jeans, rolled half way up her calf and a blue and white sear–sucker blouse tied in a mid–drift. She pulled her hair into a ponytail and went to the kitchen. Once there, her mother excused herself to lie down, stating she believed she could rest now that her children were home. Irene playfully shoved Gus out of the kitchen telling him to go to the front porch; she would serve lunch out there because it was too hot to eat inside. As Irene opened the screen door to the front porch, she saw Curly! She almost dropped the pitcher of lemonade and sandwiches. He noticed and rushed to her rescue. His hands cupped hers and although the pitcher was safe, she was weak in the knees. Curly took the tray and set it on the table, then turned and kissed her. Gus took the hint taking his sandwich and lemonade out in the yard so they could be alone. Irene didn't notice Gus's disappearance, as usual when she was in

Curly's arms there was no one else in the world. She didn't even remember to ask why he was in court! She was in his arms and that was all that mattered. They sat in the swing eating lunch. When they had finished eating, he asked if she would like to go with him to his sister's wedding. He told her he thought it was time she met his mother. Irene was so happy she answered by throwing her arms around him and planting a kiss on his waiting lips. The wedding would take place in August at his parent's home in Georgia.

Irene looked a little distraught, Curly picking up on the negative vibes asked, "What's wrong?" "I don't have anything to wear to something that special," she replied. "Don't worry, Babe. You know I'll take care of you. Besides the wedding is nearly a month away." Irene snuggled up to him as he placed his arm around her. They sat in contented silence until Gus came back on the porch, "We better get going, Cal is due back soon." Curly kissed Irene one last time, then he and Gus left. She watched as they drove out of sight, sad he was gone, but happy they would be together again soon.

The wedding was held in a beautiful garden. The foliage was crisp and the flowers were in full bloom sporting a myriad of colors. The tables were dripping in pink lace cloths and centered with replicas of the bridal bouquet. White tulle bows were tied to the back of each chair.

The bride and groom stood beneath a pink rose covered trellis to take their scared vows. Irene was pretending she and Curly were saying them, too. She was almost afraid to have those thoughts, as she feared he might not have the same intentions. After the vows were spoken everyone took their seats. Irene and Curly took a table under a magnificent magnolia tree putting them slightly out of the limelight. As they ate, Curly told her about the different characters in his family. None of them were as interesting to Irene as the men dressed in ordinary suits taking down tag numbers. She couldn't resist the temptation to ask why they were doing that. Curly shrugged and said, "It's the FBI, Edgar's a nosy son of a bitch." About this time a regal lady with graying hair, sculptured features, piercing blue eyes, wearing a stunning pink dress strolled over to the table. Irene thought she was almost as pretty as the bride! Suddenly, Curly was on his feet, "Mother, this is Irene Scott. I thought it was high time you two met," he announced. Irene extended her hand, but it went unnoticed. Irene withdrew her hand and blushed with embarrassment as his mother said, "My dear, how good of you to come. I'm sorry I won't have time to visit with you, perhaps my son will be good enough to bring you around again when things are not quite so...shall we say, festive. I always enjoy meeting one of Curly's girls, his taste in beauty is impeccable." Irene was so caught off guard by this woman's presence, as well as, her words, she didn't know how to respond. Finally she said, "Thank you for having me. I look forward to seeing you again sometime." Mrs. Glisson walked away before she even finished her sentence. Irene hoped she didn't sound as angry or look as rattled as she felt. She knew by the look on Curly's face his mother's words and attitude had infuriated him as well. She decided to pretend she didn't notice how his mother had behaved or what she had said. She could tell Curly was embarrassed by the redness of his face, and she knew in her heart he had not made a habit of carrying women to meet his mother. She smiled at him, he smiled back, and everything was as it should be.

Curly pointed to the dance floor, his mother was dancing with a tall, dark haired man, much younger than Curly. She thought perhaps he was Curly's brother. He explained his name was Joe Allums and that his family had taken him in when the boy was about ten years old. He said Joe wasn't his blood brother, but he couldn't have been closer to him had he been. Then he stood up, extended his arm to her and led her to the dance floor. The music permeated the sweet smelling air as they danced to the slow tune the orchestra was playing. When the music stopped, they went to congratulate the happy couple, "This is my girl, Irene," he said proudly. Her heart nearly leapt out of her chest at his pronouncement. She finally heard him define their relationship. She was as happy as the bride and prettier in her rose colored silk dress with pearl buttons. Her shoes were peau de soie, dyed to match her dress. She carried rose–colored lace gloves and a purse to match her shoes. Her hair was pulled up from the sides with pearl combs, and hung down her back curling slightly on the ends.

Before leaving the party Irene asked, "May I see the house?" "Oh, sure…why not?" he answered as he took her hand and led her inside.

The house was spectacular! The red carpeted winding staircase, the elaborate chandeliers, and antique furniture was reminiscent of the old moneyed antebellum homes in the South. There were more bedrooms upstairs than Irene could count, and each one had it's own bath and walk–in dressing room. One bedroom was a nursery, where a baby was sleeping. The room had a French door that led to a balcony overlooking the grounds where the wedding party was taking place. "Whose baby is this?" she whispered. "It's my sister's," he corrected himself, "My other sister, not the one getting married!" they laughed as quietly as possible. "Come on we better get out of here before it wakes up," he said as he took her hand and playfully dragged her out of the room.

They left the wedding in a limousine for the airport and journey back to Tamp. When they arrived Curly's car was waiting at the airport; Irene thought Curly was taking her home; instead he stopped at a restaurant where he had reserved the entire dining room. The table was set with a white lace cloth, dripping candles, and a dozen red roses. A bottle of Dom Pe'rignon was chilling in a silver ice bucket. Irene asked playfully, "Where's the bride and groom?" "We're here," he replied softly. He took her in his arms, waltzed her to the jukebox kicking it, soft music began to play. After dinner, they held each other, dancing until daybreak. He whispered, "Will you?" "Will I what?" she replied. She wanted him to say the words she had longed to hear for what seemed her entire life. "You're not going to make it easy on me are you, Babe?" he said smiling. "No, I'm afraid not!" she answered. "I love you. Will you marry me, Irene?" He kissed her as she finished answering, "Yes!" she had never been so happy! She couldn't help wondering however, what her family would think about her marrying

Curly. She knew her mother thought he was too old for her, but liked him otherwise, and Gus seemed to like him, but Cal was a different story! She had never discussed Curly with him, she knew not to. Whatever their differences they would have to put them aside when she and Curly married! Curly told her there was no need upsetting either family by telling them of their intentions. He felt it would be better if they told them after the fact. Irene had always dreamed of a wedding like Curly's sister's, but she didn't really mind eloping. She didn't care as long as she was married to her Curly.

Curly walked Irene to the corner, watched as she crossed the street and went into the house. The city was just coming to life. Irene should have been tired and ready to sleep, but the adrenaline was rushing in anticipation of their next encounter that would lead them to matrimony. Curly had wanted them to get married immediately, but his 'family' needed him to make trips to Texas, California, and Washington D.C., their plans had to be postponed for almost six months! Curly sent messages to her occasionally, she could not answer because she had no address for him. She had a hard time finding enough to do to keep her busy until his return. She wondered if he was feeling the same anxiousness. He was.

The day Curly was due back, Irene was like a worm in hot ashes. She prayed Cal and Gus would not be home before she left. Her mother was beginning to act suspicious, but didn't question her. Irene slipped into her mother's room, opened her top dresser drawer, and took the yellowed lace handkerchief she had carried on her own wedding day. She would explain about the handkerchief when she returned. Irene kissed her mother on the cheek and left. She had thrown her dress bag

and overnight bag out her bedroom window. Curly was waiting impatiently in his car. Irene quickly retrieved her things and darted across the street to him. Meanwhile, Mrs. Scott, sensing what was about to take place, looked in the half opened drawer and discovered her lace handkerchief was missing. She cried with mixed feelings.

Their trip began just as the moon was beginning to shine. Curly stopped at a filling station and Irene changed clothes. She had bought a beautiful white lace tea length dress, with matching pumps. She wore her hair pinned up; some naturally fell around her face and down the back of her neck. She looked stunning as she walked back to the car. Curly's face lit up like a Christmas tree when he saw her. When she got in the car he said shaking his head, "You look unbelievable! How did I get so lucky?" "I'm the lucky one," she replied as they embraced. The ride made Irene sleepy. She laid her head in his lap and quickly drifted off to sleep. The next thing she knew, she was standing face to face with a Justice of the Peace, saying, "I do." Irene never even knew what state they were in, she just knew she was finally married to the man she had loved since she was thirteen years old!

The sun was barely peeking above the horizon as they pulled into the parking space in front of their motel room. Curly unlocked the door and took the bags inside. He came back to the car for Irene. As they approached the door, Curly stopped and kissed her. They had barely closed the door before ripping each other's clothes off. Irene had never known this kind of lust, passion, love, she had only imagined how it would be, and her imagination didn't do it justice! This man knew what he was doing as he showed the tender side of himself. He was gentle as he took the part of her she chose to give to only one man, her soul. His very touch made he shiver, his kisses made her body ooze liquid fire as she found herself screaming, wanting more. She was afraid he would stop; she prayed he wouldn't, as his body pounded her very soul. She was intoxicated with love and he was drunk with the smell of her body and the silky feel of her smooth skin. Their breathless bodies stiffened for the release of six years of penned up craving for each other. They lay crying in each other's arms until they slept.

CHAPTER THREE

Several days later the newly weds returned to Tampa. Irene was nervous about her family's reaction to the marriage, especially Cal. Curly assured her it would be all right, he would see to it. She wanted to ask him the reasoning behind his and Cal's feuding, but she knew her questions would not be welcomed. She preferred to keep her marriage, their relationship, separate from any other. As long as Curly was safe, the rest didn't matter, she knew she was better off not knowing about things she couldn't change.

She was surprised when Curly parked the car in front of the Saratoga Bar! It was too early for a drink she thought; still she didn't say anything. Curly jumped out, ran around the car to open the door for his bride. Still believing they were stopping in the bar for a shot of courage before facing her family, she smiled as he took her hand leading her around to the trunk to retrieve their things. Then they walked around to the back of the Saratoga, and he trotted her up the stairs. When they reached the top, he put the bags down, unlocked the door, lifted her into his arms, and carried her over the threshold. "This is not much…and it's not permanent," he began. Irene placed her fingertips over his lips to stop his words, "It's home because you are here," she whispered. Closing the door with his foot, he kissed her and laid her on the bed. His breath on her skin made her hot. As he placed his body over hers and pressed his hardness inside her she anticipated the warm explosion that would make her shriek with joy and satisfaction. As they lay in each other's arms afterward, Irene attempted to describe to him her plans for their 'little love hut', as she called it. Just hearing her enthusiasm excited him again. He interrupted her as he began kissing her neck, her shoulder, her breast, and…she was wild with desire, he ached to consume her; They were both satisfied.

"I'm going to build you a house, Irene. A big house with a swimming pool!" he said excited. Pretending to pout, more to keep him from feeling bad about the apartment than anything else, she replied, "I like this one!" He put his arm around her and kissed her, "God, I love you!" "I love you, too. That's all that matters, she whispered.

As Curly showered, Irene mused in peaceful bliss as she continued planning the fix up of their new little home.

To most people, the little apartment might have seemed no more than a cheap efficiency motel room, but to Irene it was heaven on earth. When she looked at it she didn't see bare walls and cheap furnishings. She saw a quaint little love nest with red and white gingham curtains, white chenille bedspread, and trinkets she and Curly would pick out together. She pictured flowering plants inside and out, and on the little stoop a bamboo mat would welcome guests. She looked forward to doing all the little things that made a house a home, being the wife her husband deserved. She wanted everyone to know how happy she and Curly were, and maybe even be a tiny bit jealous of them! She longed for the time they would be a family of three, four, or maybe even five!

When Curly finished his shower he told Irene they should go visit her mother. He wanted to let Mrs. Scott know he respected her and her daughter. He felt she would consider it improper, slipping Irene off in the night. He intended for her to know his intentions were strictly honorable. He realized his relationship with Cal could never be any more than it was now. He knew what Cal was and Cal knew who he was. His fight was not with Mrs. Scott, and he had no intentions of severing the ties that bound Irene and her mother. He respected them both too much for that, and secretly wished he had the same respect for his own mother.

Mrs. Scott was a loving and forgiving lady. However, she was capable of showing her disappointment. The look in her mother's eyes was what Irene dreaded most. She had seen it before, for Cal and Gus, this time she was afraid would be the first time she had caused it. Curly understood this and assured her he would take full responsibility and everything would be fine.

While Irene showered and dressed, Curly went downstairs to the bar, and joined Gus who was sitting in a booth. Gus, being inebriated confided that Cal had gone on a gun run for Trafficante, but would be back later that afternoon. Curly called the apartment to tell Irene to meet him at the car, and they left.

Mrs. Scott greeted them with open arms. She cried a little when Irene took the lace handkerchief from her purse and handed it to her. They laughed, and then Mrs. Scott took Curly's hand and welcomed him to the family. He kissed her hands and apologized for the elopement. She stopped him in mid–sentence, "You need not explain, son. Just take care of my Irene, make her happy, that's all I want. Well, that and a few grand children," she said smiling. Curly assured her she had nothing to fear in either regard, and she believed him. He excused himself, "I'm going to let you visit alone with your mother for awhile. I promised Gus I would come back and have a drink with him. I'll be back soon." "Thanks, Curly. You're so thoughtful. I really did miss her." He kissed her and left.

Gus was sitting at the bar when Curly got there. Mikey Michaels the owner of the Saratoga poured Curly a scotch. Holding up his glass Mikey made a toast, "To the newlyweds!" All customers raised their glasses in unison and repeated Mikey's toast. About that time Cal walked in, "Who got married?" Gus slithered off the bar stool and ducked in the restroom, as Cal said louder, "Well, who the hell got married?" "I did." Curly answered. "So, what's the big damn deal? Who the hell did you marry the queen?" he snickered. "No, better than the queen. Your sister!" Curly replied. Suddenly a hush fell over the bar. "The hell you say! My sister has more sense than to marry an old fart like you!" he said disbelieving Curly. "Well, she did, last week," Curly stated. Cal picked up a chair and headed towards Curly. "All right boys, take it outside." Mikey ordered. Laying his glasses on the bar Cal replied, "Yeah, you damn right we'll take it outside! I'm fixin' to beat the shit out of this lying fat fart!" "I'm not lying. I swear to you, we got married last week." "Stop! Stop! Lying!" Cal retorted, "My sister wouldn't marry a bastard old enough to be her grandpa!" Once on the outside Curly said, "Why don't you cool off, Cal? I don't want to fight you. That doesn't honor your mother or Irene. Hell, we're kin now!"

Cal, gritting his teeth, "Don't you call my sister by her name, you asshole! Leave my mama out of this! And damn it, we're not kin!" Cal moved closer to Curly and punched him. Curly slapped him back with the palm of his hand hitting Cal's right cheek and the back of his hand coming back across his face on the left. Cal was stunned as Curly said, "Now Cal, we need to put our differences aside." Cal lunges at Curly, "The only thing I'm gonna put aside is my damn fist upside your fucking head!" By now the bar had emptied to watch the fight, including a police officer. Mikey asked the officer, "Aren't you going to do something?" He answered, "Nah, it'll all be over with in a minute. You know I can't interfere in 'family' business. My money is on Cal. How about it, you want in?" Mikey laughed, "Yeah, I'll put fifty on the Stooge!"

Both Cal and Curly were bleeding. Curly worse. Cal had Curly penned down, holding his hands above his head, with one hand, and hitting him in the ribs with the other. Curly managed to free himself from Cal and pulled a 'Stooges' act on him, poking him in the eye, running around him yelling, "Whoop, whoop", then boped him on the head with his fist! This act brought Cal to his knees. Someone helped Cal back into the bar. Curly staggered upstairs to the apartment.

Meanwhile, Gus went home and plopped down on the couch. Mrs. Scott told Irene to set the table for supper. "Gus, where's Curly? Isn't he coming to eat?" Irene questioned. "Uh…he was still at the bar when I left. He had some business to take care of," he answered.

As Irene, Gus, and Mrs. Scott sat down to eat, Cal came in nursing bleeding knuckles and bragging about what he had done, "I just beat the hell out of that son of a bitch you call your husband!" Irene was so furious she couldn't speak! Mrs. Scott was visibly upset over Cal's action and his vulgar speech. Cal continued to speak, "You better tell that fat son of bitch to stay out of my sight! I'll beat his sorry ass to a pulp every time I see him!" Just as the last word passed his lips, Mrs. Scott cold cocked him with her cane! Irene ran out of the house slamming the screen behind her. She ran all the way to the apartment. On every step was more blood than the one before it. She took a deep breath before opening the door, afraid of what she would find. Curly was slumped at the kitchen table trying to bandage himself. He looked frightful! Both eyes were swollen and turning various shades of black and blue. He had a deep gash on the left cheek, Irene was afraid it might leave another scar. His knuckles, like Cal's were bursting open and bleeding. He winced as Irene poured alcohol over his wounds. "Curly, please let me take you to the hospital!" Irene pleaded. "I…I…can't. The publicity…I can't!" He accidentally hit his hand on the edge of the table, jumping he felt pain in his ribs, "Damn it! I can't afford the publicity and neither can my family." His speech was labored with pain. Irene pulled up his shirt to reveal the swelling and bruising of his rib area. She was convinced his ribs were broken. She helped him to bed. "What happened between you and my brother?" she asked as she pulled the covers over him. "It's complicated", he groaned, "I guess we both just love his little sister too much." "Then you should have hugged each other! This is no way to prove either of you love me! Love and…this should not be used in the same sentence!" she exclaimed angrily.

A few hours later Gus brought Curly some pain pills that Cal had gotten when Gus carried him to the hospital, and some chicken soup. Irene loved her brothers, but this time she was having her say to Cal. He was not going to ruin her life! She was glad her mother had knocked him upside the head; she planned to do the same just as soon as he saw him!

When Curly was better, he made plans to take his bride on a three—month cruise on the *Carabella*. Irene was ecstatic! She was happier than she ever imagined she could be!

Before the trip got underway, Curly received word from his mother to come to Georgia…alone. Irene was angry because her mother–in law did-n't want her to come, "I knew she didn't approve of me! At your sister's wedding she was cold and hateful. I hoped we could become friends, but she won't even give me a chance!" Curly tried to calm her, "She was probably telling me not to bring Joe. She likes him, but he isn't really kin. My uncle is the one that raised him, not her. Hell, she probably doesn't even know we're married, Irene." She felt a little better and looked at him with her pouting face, they laughed.

Irene knew she would never have the relationship with Curly's mother she would like to have had. She knew Curly didn't have great expectations for her relationship with his mother either, so like with Cal, the less they were exposed to each other the better.

Curly left the next morning. Irene stayed busy visiting her mother, shopping for the apartment, decorating, and working on her songs, packing, and most of all missing her husband. The week passed more quickly than she had anticipated.

Curly had hired Gus to cook on the yacht for their cruise. He picked Irene up at the apartment to meet Curly at the marina.

Curly was on deck as they came down the pier, "Ahoy, beautiful married lady." He yelled to her as soon as she was in sight. He helped her aboard and kissed her. Gus playfully socked him on the shoulder as he got aboard, and then took his place in the galley.

Irene had no idea where they were going. She didn't care as long as Curly was with her, besides she didn't want to spoil his surprise by asking. The first night brought back memories of a few years ago when their love was new and not yet consummated. She knew this trip would be better because their lovemaking was so wonderfully unbridled. Nothing could be more perfect. She wasn't disappointed.

They cruised about ninety miles and dropped anchor. Irene had no idea where they were, night had fallen and she could see lights of what appeared to be an island. She asked pointing, "What is that over there?" Curly responded, "Cuba. The lights are pretty aren't they? I thought you would enjoy the view our first night out." "You're so romantic," she said as she kissed him. He swooped her into his arms and carried her to their cabin where the most incredible lovemaking occurred for hours! Irene's liqui-dated body lay sleeping under the covers as Curly slipped out. Irene awoke several hours later to find him missing. She slipped her negligee' on and went to the galley for a glass of juice. She heard Gus snoring as she made her way to the deck. The dingy was gone! She wondered what Curly was thinking going off alone, at night in that thing! She tried to wait for his return, but was too sleepy and cold. She retreated to the cabin where she fell fast asleep. When she awoke the next morning Curly was asleep beside her. She wondered if she had dreamed his disappearance. She decided to wait for him to mention it just in case it was a dream. She reached for her negligee' and it wasn't where she thought she had put it, instead her robe and matching slippers had replaced it. I must have been dreaming, she thought. I'm glad I was dreaming; Curly had no business in Cuba!

Gus had cooked a delicious breakfast with sausage, eggs, biscuits and coffee. Curly was excitedly discussing the remainder of their trip. They cruised the Caribbean Islands, occasionally docking for several days. Irene's favorite stop was St. Thomas, where they spent most of their time.

On the trip home, Curly told her the reason for his mother wanting to see him. He had to leave for Sicily as soon as they returned. He explained that he had no choice but to go on behalf of his Uncle Guido. His father was ill and his mother was never allowed to conduct family business, nei-ther was his father; and besides, his mother would never leave his father's side anyway.

Uncle Guido was old and could no longer make family trips. Excitedly Irene asked, "When do we leave? Are we going by boat, flying, what? Oh, Curly Sicily!" "Wait, Irene, you don't understand, we are not leaving, just me. You can't go this time."

Irene began to cry, "Why can't Joe go? He isn't old or sick, and you said yourself your uncle raised him and he is like your real brother. He could go, couldn't he?" she asked. "No, I'm sorry, Babe. I wish I didn't have to go, but I have no choice. I learned a long time ago not to worry about what you can't help. You need to learn that, too. Let's not let this ruin the rest of our trip. Let's enjoy the time we have left. I really resent it when my family messes up my good time. Come on Irene, cut me some slack." He began to tickle her; she moved away. "Look, Curly, I know you have an obligation to your family, I understand that…to a point. I don't understand why I can't go with you. You conduct business with me around all the time. I don't interfere, I wouldn't. So, why can't I go with you?" she almost begged. "It's too dangerous. I can't explain and I don't like being given the third degree! You cannot go and that's the end of it! Now, we can both put this behind us and enjoy the rest of the trip, or you can continue sulking and make it fucking miserable for both of us! I rather have a peaceful, loving time with my wife than this bullshit, now which is it?" She didn't give him an answer as she went to their cabin. He stood it as long as he could, then he followed her. "Look Irene," he said as he opened the door. She was waiting patiently for him, in the nude, sitting in the middle of the bed. She said not a word, just motioned, 'come hither' with her finger. He didn't have to be asked twice!

Irene dreaded the day the yacht docked. It wouldn't be but a couple of days now. She knew every crash of the waves brought them closer to home and closer to his leaving. She didn't feel three months was long enough for a couple to spend together before having to be separated. He had said his mother wouldn't leave her husband, but Curly was expected to leave his wife! She couldn't see the fairness in that at all! It might not be so bad if Sicily were not half way around the world, and if he knew when he would be back! She began to feel queasy and wished he had waited to tell her this nightmare when they got home! She hated to let him see her anguish, she knew it was his business and she had to stay out of it. She didn't feel well enough that evening to dine with him at the table. so he had Gus make chicken soup for her, and he served her in bed. He fluffed her pillows and fed her soup. Later, he held her all night long. She knew she was the luckiest woman in the world and she felt sorry for every other woman alive!

The next night was the last night of their trip. Irene was feeling some better as she dressed for dinner. Curly had her favorite Schnapps, Gus had prepared bacon wrapped filet mignons, and the table was set with fine china and candles. A perfect setting, a perfect marriage, a perfect life...

When the yacht docked Curly was talking to the captain, paying him and Gus. Irene waited on the pier for Curly. He escorted her back to their apartment, and took her in his arms, "Irene, I love you no matter what. Just because you might not hear from me for a while, doesn't mean I've stopped caring or that I'm sick or hurt. It just means I'm very busy, that's all." He kissed her, and she held on as tight as she could. They both wanted more and even though he was in a hurry, he forgot all about family business, deadlines, and anything else, but her. They made mad passionate love and when it was over he showered, redressed and sat down on the bed. "I have paid for the apartment until I return. The grocery store is running a tab. Mikey will see you get a taxi whenever you need one." He bent down and kissed her on the forehead, "I love you, Irene." He left.

She continued to bask in the warm afterglow of their love until it ozzed out of her body and left her cold, just as his leaving had. She cried for three days as she tried to convince herself he wouldn't be gone long. She couldn't seem to keep anything on her stomach; she was just too upset!

CHAPTER FOUR

As time passed and there had been little word from Curly, Irene had to keep reminding herself he was just busy, as he had said.

When Irene's queasiness continued, she made an appointment with the doctor where she learned she was expecting a baby. She was so happy yet, not having heard from Curly made her sad. She cried all the way home because he wasn't there to share this wonderful time with her. As the taxi turned the corner she held her breath in hopes he would be standing on the stairs of the apartment waiting for her return. She let out her breath in exasperation when he wasn't. She wanted to share the news with her mother, but she really wanted Curly to be the first to know. She decided to wait awhile before telling anyone. She just knew he would be home soon.

Three months passed with no word from her beloved. She was afraid her little secret was beginning to show. She made up her mind to tell her mother she was expecting a baby. Before Irene could tell her the news, Mrs. Scott smiled, "OH…a baby! When's it coming, Irene?" Irene was flabbergasted that her mother knew without her saying a word, "Mama! Does it show that much?" Her mother laughed aloud as she hugged her. Then Irene began to cry, "Mama, I just know Curly isn't coming back! It's been nearly four months and I haven't heard a word from him. Oh, Mama what am I'm going to do?" "Now, Irene you just stop that! Curly loves you. He's just busy that's all. Men don't think like women, honey. Why I remember when your Papa would go out on the shrimp boats. Sometimes I wondered if he had drowned and nobody told me! I didn't ever know if he'd make it home in time for you children to be born! He always did, and Curly will too. You just mark my words. He'll be back." She comforted her as best she could, listening as she talked and holding her as she cried. "But Mama, he doesn't even know about the baby yet. I haven't heard from him to tell him. That's why I haven't told you about the baby before now. I didn't want anyone to know before I told him." "I know, honey. Sometimes we don't get what we want. Why don't you come stay with me until Curly comes back?" "I can't, Mama! That would be like giving up! Admitting Curly was gone forever! I just can't, Mama."

Time passed slowly, as day after day, she waited for Curly, a phone call, a letter, anything!

One day there was a knock at the door. Irene opened it with excitement, thinking it was Curly. It wasn't, instead, Joe Allums was standing on the landing bearing a dozen yellow roses and a message from Curly, *Joe is going to take care of you until my return. I love you, C.'* Irene smiled. "Curly says you're going to take care of me. You'll be staying here?" Shyly Joe replied, "The sofa will be fine. If that's ok with you." "Won't you have a seat…on your new bed? Curly has told me all about you, Joe. I'm sorry we haven't met before now." "Yeah, me too. Curly wishes he was here. He hates being gone so long, but duty calls." Irene stood, "Yeah, that's what he said, but I sure do miss him, especially now." She rubbed her big stomach and they both laughed. Picking up her handbag, "I promised my mother I would come by today. I shouldn't be gone too long. Make yourself at home." "Oh, why don't you let me drive you? My car's right outside." "Thanks, but I didn't know you were coming, I've called a taxi." She gave him a wave as she waddled down the stairs. For the first time in six months Irene felt happy, relieved, and alive!

She wasn't sure what to do with Joe; she didn't quite know how to handle the situation. She wasn't sure how it would look to people having a man that wasn't her husband staying in the same apartment with her. She talked to her mother about it over coffee, "Mama, what would you do?" "Curly's your husband, honey, and right now he is doing the very best he knows how to take care of you. People need to mind their own business, don't worry about what they think. Just know you are doing what your husband wants, he's the one you have to please." Irene decided she was right. She would treat him as if he were Curly's brother.

Joe proved to be a great friend. Irene was glad he was there. He refused to let her lift a finger. He cooked, cleaned, took out the garbage, ran errands, took her to and from the doctor, whatever she needed. He spoiled her just like she knew Curly would, had he been there.

When Irene was beginning her ninth month of pregnancy, Curly returned from Sicily. He knocked on the door trying not to act surprised at Irene's condition, but finally he said he wasn't expecting her to be that far along. He did not take her in his arms as she had anticipated. Instead, he stepped inside, shook hands with Joe and asked him to go down to the bar awhile. Joe did as he asked, leaving them alone. Curly took her hand, seating her on the sofa. He sat at the other end. It were if he were visiting instead of being in his own home. He was scaring Irene. For the first time since they married she felt as if he were a stranger. Finally, he moved just close enough to place his hand on her stomach to feel the baby kicking. Tears came to his eyes as he began to speak, "Irene, I have something to tell you. It's the hardest thing I have ever had to tell anyone, so I may stumble a little, but it has to be said. First of all, let me say that there is nothing I can do about the situation, no matter how much I want to. You must know that I love you and the baby, but you also know I have an obligation to my 'family', and those obligations have always had to come first in my life. When my family found out we were married my departure was arranged." Irene started to speak, "Please, Irene let me say what I have come here to say. Irene…our marriage has been annulled! There! I've said it. I'm sorry, but I can't do anything about this, it would place you and the baby in too much danger, and I love you too much to let that happen. I hate what my family stands for! I hate the fact that my wants and needs never come first." Irene just sat there listening, in shock. "I went against them when I married you on two counts. First of all, you're Cal's sister and second, you are not Catholic." In a stunned voice Irene asked, "What does Cal have to do with it?" "Cal works for a family that for the most part my family hates. Since a priest did not marry us in a Catholic Church, our marriage was never recognized by the Church. It's as if we were never married! Now, he has gone to the Pope and had annulment papers drawn up. Hell, he has everybody from the Pope to the postman in his pocket, anyway. Now, because he feels I have betrayed my family and God, I have to agree to sign whatever legal papers and all the bullshit that goes with it, or he'll see to it we all die! I swear to you, one day I will get even for this...no matter what!" Irene felt her blood pressure rising, she could feel her heart beating in her head, and the baby was kicking, as she asked, "What are you telling me? Are you saying you're leaving me, Curly?" Reluctantly and with his head bowed, he turned away as he replied, "Yes, I guess I am." His voice sounded wimpy to Irene. She had never heard him sound that way and it made her furious he chose now to become a cowed down 'Mama's Boy'! "Well, what do you propose I do, Curly? I am carrying your child! Your family can't annul that! Or can they? This child was not conceived out of wedlock; it's not some back alley love child, Curly! It's your baby! It's our baby, it's..." tears began streaming down her cheeks. He turned to face her. He wanted to take her in his arms, but he knew if he did, he would never let her go. He pleaded, "I'm so sorry, Irene. I love you. I just can't take the chance. I shouldn't confide this to you, but I have to so you'll know I am telling you the truth. They killed Joe's wife and little girl because he disobeyed their request, and hell he's not even blood related! He married a girl that had a great–great uncle in a rival 'family', and he was the last one in her family to participate in an organization. The rest of her family had no idea this man that had been dead for years, had ever been in an organization! They hold grudges, Irene. They don't care who gets in their way! Please. I know you're upset, but don't mention this to Joe. If he tells you, that's his business, but don't you bring it up. We can't choose the families we are born into, Irene. You know that. I would lay my life down for you or the baby, but I'll be damned if I will sacrifice either of you just to stay married!" he knelt beside her, "Somehow, I will see you and the baby, but I cannot sign your death warrant...I can't, and damn it

I won't?" He stood, took his hat and opened the door. When he was on the porch he turned to her, "I have to do what they want." Still angry and scared she replied, "You go ahead, do what they want you to, you...you Mama's boy! Then she slapped him across the face, hard. In reflex he slapped her back! She lost her footing and plunged down the stairs! "Irene!" he yelled, as he went to where she lay trying to see that she was all right. He was scared and angry with himself. He wanted to grab her up and tell her how sorry he was, that he didn't mean it, but again, he knew he wouldn't be able to let her go, and he had to. Joe walked up just about the time Curly got to Irene, Curly saw him. "It was an accident, Joe. I'd never hurt her like this!" he said with tears in his eyes. He looked down at her lying there, calling his name and reaching for him. He pulled off his wedding ring and threw it as far as he could throw it, as he ran down the remaining steps. Irene was screaming for him, but he kept going, leaving Joe to pick up the pieces and Irene.

Joe put Irene to bed and tried to calm her down. She continued to cry, begging him. "Please, Joe! Go find him; he's hurting! Please, find him, Joe and tell him I love him! Please, hurry!" "Irene I can't leave you after a fall like that! He'll be back and he'll be all right, he always is. Just calm down, now." Still crying uncontrollably, "Not this time! He's not all right! Please Joe. I'll be fine, I promise. Please, please!" she begged. "All right! Calm down. I'll go, but I'll be back soon. Don't move, Irene. I mean it, stay in bed!" he ordered. "I will, Joe. I promise, please hurry!"

Joe was gone almost two hours, searching every bar and joint he thought Curly would go, and a few he wouldn't. No luck. When he returned, Irene was in labor. He grabbed her and ran as fast as he could to the car. He put her in the back seat and sped away, doing the maximum his car would allow. They made it just in time! Irene delivered a beautiful, healthy baby girl with a little round face, and lips just like her father! Curly wasn't there.

CHAPTER FIVE

The birth of their daughter was a mixed blessing for Irene. She was devastated about her marriage, yet she was so thankful for the child that represented the love she and Curly had for one another.

She knew no matter how their last meeting ended, Curly loved her and the baby. She believed him when he said he feared for their safety, that fear must have been equal to the love he had for them or, he would have stayed. As badly as she wanted to hate him, she couldn't, not yet.

The nurse brought in a beautiful arrangement of two–dozen pink roses. The handwritten card read, *'Forgive me. God knows I love you both. She's beautiful, as is her mother. I hope you will think about the little girl I told you about and consider naming our baby after her, 'Jacqueline'. Joe has been good to us; thank him for me. I'm sorry for everything. I love you both, C'.*

Irene cried as she read the card, somehow it made it all final. He wasn't coming back, at least not for good. She knew she would live for the day she would see him again. She was back where she started. They had taken ten steps forward only to be pushed back ten! She hated the thoughts of having to love that way, but it beat the alternative! She was his wife in her heart and nobody could annul that, she would remain faithful to him forever.

Irene allowed Joe to read Curly's card. She didn't want to bring up what Curly had told her, but she was afraid naming the baby after his little girl would upset him. He read the card with tears in his eyes, "I'm honored Irene, that Curly thinks that much of me and that you would consider doing this. Thank you." He hugged her for the first time ever, then said, "What are your plans now?" Irene shrugged, "I don't have any, really. Just to raise my baby, keep loving Curly, and take it one day at a time like before we were married. I don't have any other choice." "Curly really does love you, Irene. He's just a stooge sometimes in more ways than one! I've known him a long time and I've never seen him as happy as he has been since he met you. He is in a situation that could cause problems. He can't take that chance, Irene. Don't hate him. I know it's not over for the two of you. It never will be. Just remember that, when you start doubting him." "I know what you are saying is the truth, Joe, but does it have to hurt so bad?" He patted her hand and said, "It will get better, I promise. I'll run over to the apartment and pick up what you need for a few days, until you can decide what you are going to do. I know your mother would like for you to come there." Irene gasped, "Mama! Has anyone told Mama about the baby?" "Yeah, Curly went to see her to explain things. He also sent a crib and some other things you'll need for the baby. Oh, and here is some money. He said he would send more, later. It's going to be all right, Irene. You'll see." She nodded. For the first time, in what seemed years, Irene smiled. "Thanks, Uncle…Joe!" she said playfully as the nurse brought the baby in.

Her mother was so excited about having a baby in the house! Gus was there when they arrived. "Granny, Uncle Gus, meet Jacqueline Olivia Glisson!" Irene announced proudly. Her mother took the baby and kissed her from head to toe! Gus didn't know what to say to Irene about Curly. He knew the situation, who Curly was, and had figured it would end like this one day. He like Irene, dreaded what Cal would have to say, but unlike Gus, Irene had decided she wasn't going to take anything off of him.

Just as Irene put the baby down, Cal came in. He looked in the crib, "Damn! She looks just like that son of bitchin' daddy of her's! Couldn't you have done something about that?" He laughed. Irene slapped him as hard as she could! He was so shocked by her actions he couldn't do anything! "The longest day you live, Calvin Scott, don't you ever refer to him like that again! You're partly to blame for my life being in the mess it's in, and for my baby having to be raised without her father! If you weren't mixed up with that Trafficante bunch, this could have been prevented. You're my brother and I can't help that! I can't help loving you either, and you had better be glad of that, but I refuse to allow you to make anymore unnecessary remarks!" She took her finger and pecked him in the chest, "You got that, Cal?" "Yeah, sis...I got it! I..." She interrupted, "Just shut up, Cal! Just shut up!" Their mother was standing there and heard the whole thing. She took her cane and lambed him across the butt with it! "Behave, Cal! And watch your mouth! You hear?"

Irene was busy with the baby and somehow found it difficult to worry about Curly. The money Curly had given her was dwindling away. She knew she would have to go to work soon.

One afternoon, while Gus was home, she asked him to help watch the baby for awhile. She went to the apartment to get the rest of her things. It was hard to walk the stairs where she had last seen Curly, but she took a deep breath and climbed them...one at a time. As she reached the door she was taken aback because the door was ajar. She took her foot and pushed it open. The flat was empty, except for a few boxes, which were stacked in a corner. There was not much left of the life and love she had known just a few months earlier, and would never know again. She walked through the emptiness, then sat in the middle of the living room floor and sobbed. Her leaking breasts gave her a reminder that it was time to go. She walked out leaving behind the best part, her heart. There would never be a man she could love as she had Curly, and she knew, he knew it as well. Deep down, she believed he felt the same, she just knew it.

When she returned home, she heard the baby crying and for the first time, realized her only responsibility was to her daughter. She was all she had left now, of her love for Curly. She would go on.

Irene and her mother moved to a duplex cabin at Desoto Park, where Irene found work cleaning the cabins and doing the laundry. Irene thought living in a duplex would give both her mother and herself some privacy. She was close enough to hear her mother if need be and vice versa. as long as the radio was turned down.

The baby was about nine months old now and Curly had never held her. One afternoon, Joe came around with a note that read, '*Please allow me to see you and my daughter. Love, C'.* Irene wanted to say, "NO!", but, her heart said, "YES!" and at three o'clock, Curly drove up. Irene's heart jumped up in her throat. It was pounding so hard and fast she just knew he could see it! He was dressed in a suit and tie, and was wearing a hat. As he entered the cabin, he removed the hat to reveal he had let his hair grow a bit. To Irene he was very handsome and she wanted him more right then, than she could remember. Without a word, Irene handed the baby to him. "She's beautiful, Irene, like her mother," he said softly. "She looks just like you, Curly. Everybody says you couldn't deny her," she replied. thinking, 'Yeah, but in a way he has.'

Irene noticed that he was not at all uncomfortable or fidgety around the baby. In fact, she was pleasantly surprised at the ease with which he held his little girl. He kissed her chubby cheeks and head, held his finger so she could wrap her hand around it. She laughed when he curled his lip and quipped, N'yuk, N'yuk, N'yuk at her. Irene couldn't help laughing. Curly told her his camera was in the car and asked if she minded getting it for him. As she walked to the car her gait quickened as the thought crossed her mind, he might duck out the back with the baby! She felt ashamed when she walked back to the cabin and he was playing horsey with the baby, saying a nursery rhyme as he took her hand and went down the buttons on the front of his shirt, "Rich man, poor man, beggar man, thief, doctor, lawyer, Indian chief." The baby got tickled every time he finished and held her back as if he were going to drop her in the floor.

They walked out on the porch, Curly carrying the baby. "Come down here among the trees and let me get your picture with her," Irene requested. He honored her request and she snapped the picture. He wanted one of Irene and the baby, but she began crying for her mother to feed her, so they took her back inside. Curly stayed while Irene nursed her. As she put the baby in the crib, Curly came up behind her, put his arms around her waist squeezing her to him. Irene took a deep breath as she felt his hardness pressing against her. She leaned her head against his chest, hoping he would take her as he had so many times before. He gently turned her to him. Their eyes met, a kiss ensued and as it was with their very first kiss the passion rose, as did their temperatures and before either realized it, they were making love. There were no inhibitions, no reservations. They were meant to be. It had been so since their first meeting, and it would be so, until both drew their last breath. Irene didn't want this moment to end, but it did. No sooner than Curly could regain his strength to leave, he did. As he was getting in his car, he told her he loved her and their daughter, but he wanted them to be safe, and that meant they could not live together. "I cannot be a frequent participant in your lives, Irene, but I know where you are and what is going on all the time. I'll try to be here if you ever really need me. I love you both so much." She made no remark, just took a deep breath, shook her head in disgust, turned and went inside. She refused to watch him leave.

After he left, she walked next door to check on her mother. She was listening to the radio and did not know Curly had even been there. Irene told her about Curly's visit, (most of it), and how the baby had really taken to him. Mrs. Scott smiled, Irene left to check on the baby.

Sleep did not come for her that night and she doubted she would ever be at peace again.

The next day, she tried to do the laundry for the cabins during the time the baby napped in the afternoon. She decided to finish the laundry; while it was line drying and the baby was sleeping, she would try to nap as well. She checked on her mother, she was happily listening to the radio and didn't need anything. Irene went back to her cabin and placed the baby in the bed with her. She slept topless so if the baby cried to be fed she wouldn't have to get up. She and the baby were fast asleep when suddenly the covers were jerked off, and the baby was snatched! Irene jumped up to retrieve Jacqueline. As her feet hit the floor, two other men seized her by the arms. One of them placed his hand over her mouth so she couldn't scream. It didn't keep her from biting the fatty part of his hand, he screeched! Then he slapped her so hard she nearly passed out. They dragged her to the back porch to tie her up, "You keep your mouth shut and don't call the cops or she dies!"

The suit that had his hand bitten used his head to point saying, "Hey look, a tit holder!" "What the fuck is a tit holder?" the other suit questioned. "Watch!" he said, as he grabbed Irene dragging her to the wringer washer. He shoved her breasts in the wringer and turned the handle! The pain was so horrendous Irene did pass out! As the men were leaving, one noticed the camera lying on the table by the door; he picked it up and made a picture of Irene. They left with the camera, laughing all the way to the car, "That'll teach the bitch to bite my fucking hand!" "Yeah, well, Curly's gonna teach you to fucking wring his woman's tits in a washing machine! He said we better not hurt anybody."

Irene came to as Gus was laying her on the bed. Mrs. Scott was sitting by the bed trying to find some way to help. She sent Gus to find some ice to pack Irene's breasts. The swelling had caused her nipples to crack open and bleed. The bruising was beginning and they throbbed with every beat of her heart. Irene was crying uncontrollably, saying something over and over they couldn't understand. Mrs. Scott didn't realize the baby had been taken until she went to check on her and she wasn't there. She began to cry and scream, "Irene…Irene…where's Jackie? Where's the baby?" Then she realized what Irene was trying to tell them. They wanted to call the police, but Irene was afraid, she knew in her heart Curly's family was behind it. She had no idea it was Curly acting alone.

Irene refused to go to the hospital; for one thing, she couldn't explain what had happened to her! She knew it was pretty unbelievable! And for another she knew who was behind it.

For several days, her mother continued to put ice on her breasts for the swelling and Gus brought her pain pills. Her ordeal had caused the natural flow of milk to dry up, which was a blessing for her. She cried and prayed for her daughter, which was all she knew to do until she was back on her feet again. She asked Gus to get Cal to rescue Jackie, but as usual, he was off on Trafficante business and out of pocket. Irene would have to wait a few more days and go herself.

Mrs. Scott urged Irene again to contact the authorities. She wasn't sure what she should do. She knew Curly wouldn't allow any harm to come to the baby, but then again the thought of what they had done to Joe's little girl kept running through her mind, and she would begin having doubts. She tried to do as Joe had advised, remember that Curly really loved her. It was never hard to believe that...until now. She had believed she could never miss anyone as much as she did Curly...she was wrong.

She had a hard time lying their doing nothing. She had to think of a way to get her baby back...soon!

Gus brought an old friend of Irene's to see her, Joe. As they walked in Gus found a note under Irene's door. It read, 'Baby is safe. Don't phone the authorities. The baby will have the kind of life she deserves if you do not pursue her return.'

The note was unsigned and did not have Curly's initial as did his usual correspondence. This note infuriated Irene and she was determined to get her baby back, no one would stop her, not even him!

Joe saw the look on Irene's face and asked what was going on. Irene explained all the gory details. He was almost as infuriated as Irene! "Who do you think is behind this, Joe?" she asked. "I hate to say it Irene, but you had better act fast. I would help you if I were in a position to, but I've already lost my family to them and I won't help sacrifice Curly's." "Can't you tell me anything that would help me, Joe?" she pleaded. "If they ever found out I helped you, Irene I'd be killed. I'm sorry. I had better get out of here, if you're being watched, my ass is grass already. Take care, Irene. Good luck. I'm really sorry I can't help you." With that he left. A little while later another note was slipped under the door. It read, *Rural Route nine, Peach City, Georgia. Memorize and burn!* She knew Joe had written the note, she recognized his handwriting. She burned the note in the ashtray as he had asked.

Irene heeded the warning about notifying the authorities. She knew where to look for her baby, and as soon as she could travel, she would do just that!

A week later Irene was able to stop carrying her breasts on a pillow whenever she got off the bed, but she still could not wear a bra. Her mother bound her breasts in a piece of sheet, gave her enough money for a round–trip bus ticket and Gus drove her to the station in his rattle trap car. He would stay with their mother while Irene was away. "Here," Gus said as he handed her a baby bottle, "I think this might fit in your purse." It did and Irene hugged him.

During the trip, Irene thought about how she would retrieve her baby. She remembered her mother reminding her of the mole on Jackie's face. She thought about Curly's sister's wedding and how there was a sleeping baby in an upstairs bedroom. She would begin her search there.

She was worried that she might not be successful in getting the baby the first time she tried. However, she knew if she didn't succeed the first time, she would probably never see her little girl again!

As usual, her heart had led her mind and she didn't plan financially very well. Since she had not worked in over a week, she had no pay coming. Mrs. Scott had given her what money she had, and Gus was footing the rest of the bills. She wasn't sure what she was going to do, but she knew somehow it had to work out; it just had to!

She was the first one off the bus, as she stepped down there was a dark brown leather money pouch at her feet. It contained thirty–seven dollars and twelve cents, and no identification. She clutched it to her and looked heavenward as she said, "Thank you."

With her newfound windfall, Irene hailed a taxi. "Where to little lady?" the driver asked. "Rural Route nine, the Glisson Estate," she answered "What you want to go way out there for? You got kin living out there, have you?" "Yes." She replied in a tone that gave the hint she was not interested in carrying on a conversation with him. She needed the quiet right now. They drove for what seemed an hour. When they finally stopped, she paid him and said, "I will need a ride back to the station in about forty–five minutes, can you be here?" "Yes ma'am," he answered, "I'll be here." "Blow the horn once and I'll come." "Yes ma'am."

Irene surveyed the white wooden fence for a gate and guards, there were neither. The moon came from behind a cloud illuminating the fence enough for her to see a loose board on an otherwise perfectly maintained structure. She detached the board and crossed to the other side. The grounds looked much different than the last time she was there. The wedding tents, tables, and hundreds of guests had disguised the vastness of the property. Irene scampered across the well–manicured lawn. When she reached the house; she saw the balcony a couple of floors up and an open door. She could hear a baby crying, then another, and another! A light went on in the room. When the babies had been quieted and the light went off, she shimmed up the trellis and onto the balcony. There, by the moonlight she could see three sleeping babies in a crib, all about the same size! She stood on the balcony, taking deep breaths as she surveyed the room. The door to the hallway was closed. She tiptoed across to the crib humming softly. She felt each baby's face for the mole, when she found it, she gathered the baby into her arms, using the blanket that covered her, carried Jackie out papoose style. They slithered down to the ground and dashed back across the lawn. Once out of the fence, she sat on the grass, unwrapped the baby, and looked at her as if seeing her for the very first time. She traced her face with her fingertips and counted her fingers and toes. Her little mouth was just like her daddy's. She smiled at Irene and babbled a little. Irene was so thankful to have her baby back, and that the babies had not started crying while she was there. She held Jacqueline close and sang one of her songs to her. She heard a car horn sound once. She gathered her precious bundle and they were on their way.

When they reached the bus station, she paid the fare and went inside. She bought a carton of milk for Jackie and a Baby Ruth and Coca Cola for herself.

The bus ride home was quiet and dark. As Irene held her daughter, she relived her adventure just a short time ago. As she did, she smiled and thought that Joe had done more than give her the address, that loose board was just too convenient!

CHAPTER SIX

Irene and her mother left DeSoto Park and moved to Marconi Street, closer to town. She knew she would have to find work to support her daughter, and from the note she had received about not pursuing Jackie's return, she knew she shouldn't count on regular support from Curly, and no support of any kind from his family. Although it was hard for her to believe with her mind that Curly was behind the kidnapping, she knew in her heart it was him. She knew as he had said, he wouldn't be able to "actively participate" in their lives, and taking Jackie might have been the only way he could have been near her.

Mikey Michaels the owner of the Saratoga, was a kind man, short and stout in stature. He always wore dress clothes and arrayed himself in gold jewelry. He was well aware of Irene's background, her marriage to Curly and the fact that her brother was affiliated with the Trafficante family. It was a safe assumption that Mikey was a friend to the 'families', allowing them to use his bar for various deals, including gun running and prostitution. Still, he had a heart and when Irene asked him for a job he gave her one, as a barmaid. He trained her to tend the bar as well.

Irene had been working at the Saratoga for nearly two years. She was good at what she did and the money including tips was great! Mikey treated her like family and tried to shield her from as much 'family' business as possible.

When 'family' business was being conducted in the bar, Irene had to be gotten out of the way. Jock Connolly, a tall, handsome detective with dark hair and crystal blue eyes, always seemed handy with a warrant for Irene, with charges ranging from obstruction of justice to prostitution. When these trumped up charges were made, Irene would be taken to the jail for a couple of hours or so, then she would be released, with no trial, no fines, nothing. Jock admitted to her once that the warrants were served to protect her, but he wouldn't say from whom or what, or by whose orders her protection was being provided. Sometimes she would retaliate by putting bubble bath in the fountain at the courthouse!

Once when Jock came to 'arrest' Irene, he admitted he was given orders to pick her up, and there were no real charges. She talked him out of carrying her to the station, promising to go home quietly if he would not run her in. He smiled and carried her home. As she saw the tail lights go around the corner, she slipped back to the Saratoga to watch who went in. She saw several mob members go in, including one of the men that was on the yacht when she stowed away! Her heart began to pound when she saw Curly go in, too! She wanted to go in, but she knew she would get Jock into trouble and maybe herself as well, so she resisted the urge.

Irene liked Jock; he wasn't a dirty cop, just worked for a dirty department, including the Police Chief, Mayor, District Attorney, and several other well–known attorneys around town. Jock played both sides of the fence because he had a family to feed and needed a job.

That night as she lay in bed, she felt afraid for Curly, of what he was doing in that bar. She wondered if she would ever stop caring for him. Deep in her hear she knew the answer was ‚'no'.

The next day, a note arrived under Irene's door, '2:00 a.m. apartment, Love C.' Irene began singing and dancing around, happier than she could remember! Jackie picked the note up pretending to read it, "Mama, look that says 'C'.! Who is C?" "Now how did you know that was someone?" they laughed. "C is just somebody that comes to see me once in a while, that's all." She replied dancing around with Jackie perched on her feet like a life–sized doll. "Is that why you are so happy, Mama?" "No, that's not all. I'm happy because I love you and you love me, darling!" Jackie hugged her around her waist, "Oh, Mama! I love you, too!" "Come on, you can help me get all prettied up!" Jackie watched as Irene picked out her dress. She went over to the dresser and put on some of her mother's powder and lip-stick, "Do I look beautiful like you, Mama?" she asked. "Oh, you look more beautiful than me!" Jackie didn't know how she could look more beautiful than her mama when she left that evening.

Her shift seemed longer than usual, but at 2:00a.m. she walked out back and there on the steps was Curly. They embraced as soon as they were within arms length. She was so glad to finally be in his arms again! He whisked her up the stairs to what had once been their place. It looked different from the last time she had been there. There was a couch, a bed with sheets, a radio sitting on the floor, shades on the windows her ging-ham curtains once graced, and towels in the bath.

He told her he had been to Nashville and had a surprise for her. He turned the radio on and a few minutes later the disc jockey announced he was "playing a song for Irene from her one true love."

Then, someone began singing one of her songs, one she had written!" She had a million questions about how he managed to get her song on the radio, but he didn't answer any of them. (She would never know any of the details, nor would she ever receive credit for having written it, or roy-alties from it. In later years she believed that Curly's family used her music as a way of punishment for their clandestine relationship. There would be many times she would hear one of her songs being played on the radio.)

She was so excited that her song was being played, she was in his arms and all was right with the world again.

On the table were a dozen yellow roses, a bottle of Peach Schnapps, and his bottle of Scotch. During times like these Irene seemed to forget the bad things he did to her. Besides, he always had a reasonable or romantic excuse for his deeds.

Curly took her in his arms and a kissed her. She pulled him to her and began unbuttoning his shirt and in turn he unbuttoned her dress. She playfully and seductively bit at his ear, he kissed her breast, she clawed at his back, he pressed his manhood against her and she dropped to the floor spreading her legs inviting him to take her. He did, several times.

Curly wasn't around for a while after that, at least not that Irene knew. She was hauled out many more times and every time she could talk Jock into just taking her home, she slipped back to the bar to see if Curly went in. Each time he didn't she was disappointed and relieved.

On several occasions Mikey gave her money from Curly for the baby, who by now was nearly four years old. She never asked Mikey how he got the money from Curly, she knew he was probably told not to discuss those details and she didn't want to put him on the spot. She did wish she could see Curly; she missed him terribly.

One night business was kind of slow, which was rare, especially on a Saturday. Irene knew something was happening and that Jock would be there soon to haul her out. "Mikey, I know there must be a meeting or something tonight, so could I just go on home and save Jock the trouble of 'arresting me?" They laughed, "Yeah, go on home, Irene. I'll see you Monday." With that she left, but she didn't go home. She hid underneath the stairs of the apartment so she could see who went in through the back door. Curly was the last one in; she heard the large metal lock snap after his arrival. She walked home in a daze wishing she could be with him once more, but afraid he might still want to take Jackie away. She worked herself into quite a state imagining him sending someone to snatch her again. She knew if it were to ever happen again, she would not get her little girl back. She wrestled in bed with her thoughts until she couldn't stand it any longer. She got up, went to the phone and called Jock. He came to the house as he was getting off duty and Irene asked him to please take Jackie home with him for the night and keep her safe. He reluctantly agreed, thinking she was being overly concerned. He wasn't aware that Curly had taken her before. When Jock left, she called Mikey and told him to tell Curly she needed to see him. The next morning a note was shoved under her door, *'Meet me at the Sea Breeze Restaurant for lunch, twelve o'clock, Love C'.*

Irene was like a schoolgirl getting ready for her first date. Standing in front of the mirror, she stared at a woman plagued by unrequited love for a man she knew she would never have for keeps. At times, she hated herself for loving him, but she never one time hated him. She wanted to be with him and she could hardly wait for lunchtime.

Curly sent a taxi for her. When she arrived, he was waiting for her in his car. He got out of the car and paid the fare. As the taxi pulled away, Curly turned to Irene, put his arm around her, and kissed her cheek, "It's good to see you, Babe." Smiling she replied, "You, too." Once inside and seated, he ordered hamburgers, fries, chocolate malt and two straws. They acted like teenagers on a first date. Irene could hardly eat; the old feelings were welling up inside her. He was feeling the same, and wasted no time paying the check and getting out of there!

As they walked along the dock hand in hand, he told her how much he had missed her. Each time they were together she wanted to ask him about the kidnapping, false arrests, gun running, but she didn't want to spoil their time together, and she knew discussing those things would more than likely end it. Besides, she knew the answer he had given her in California about events at the party, he would probably say the same about this.

When they reached the pier, he dropped her hand and motioned for her to wait. He walked up on the pier and met with one of the shrimpers she had seen at the Saratoga. She saw him pass Curly something and Curly hand him a roll of money. When he returned to her, they got in his car and drove to a nearby park. In the trunk, he had a chilled bottle of Peach Schnapps and a bottle of Scotch. The conversation remained light as he asked about his daughter, "I'll bet Jacqueline has really grown." "Yes, she has." That was all that was said. They kissed, listened to the radio, and drank. Drinking was more his style than hers, as she had not had a drink since the last time they were together. Not being accustomed to the liquor or the 'Mickey' he slipped in it, she became inebriated and the last thing she remembered was going into town.

When she awoke in her own bed she felt pain across her shoulder blades. She got out of bed, removed her blouse to have a look in the mirror. There in bold black letters was Curly's name! She was flabbergasted!

She sat down on the bed and on the pillow beside hers, that had once been his side of the bed, lay a single red rose and a note which read, *'In spite of what our families believe, you will always belong to me! Love C.'* In a bizarre way, this comforted her, even though a tattoo would have never crossed her mind, much less her back! She felt closer to him than she had in a very long time, and that was a good feeling.

Irene showered and dressed for work. Jock brought Jackie back just as she was about to leave. "Thanks, Jock. I don't know what got into me last night. I guess I was acting like a schoolgirl." "Don't apologize, my kids loved having her to play with. Let me know if I can ever do it again for you. My wife wants another one, so maybe if I carry Jackie home every now and then she'll get off my back!" He tipped his hat and headed down the steps. "You need a lift?" he offered. "Thanks, I appreciate it." She kissed Jackie, told her mother goodbye, and left. (Jock would come to Irene's rescue many times, taking Jackie when Irene was afraid she would be snatched or when she needed to keep Jackie safe.)

When she arrived at the Saratoga, the bar was alive with 'suits', as Mikey called them. Irene knew that was a nickname for the local mobsters. One 'godfather', Santos Trafficante, usually came to the bar only after closing, so Irene knew this must be something big. Mikey told her to just tend the bar and keep her mouth shut, "Be like the little monkey," he said making the hand motions, "See no evil, hear no evil, speak no evil." Irene nodded in understanding. She had been working about an hour when Chet Small came in. Small, a local businessman owned a service station and several shrimp boats. In the 'family' circles he was known as the 'disposer', his shrimp boats were the perfect cover when cleaning up the mob's mess. He wasn't a bad man, but like Jock, wanted to make a living for his family. He knew if he did not assist the 'families' he would be run out of business or worse. So, he did what he had to do.

Also present was Bob Margolis, the Mayor of Tampa who had his hat in the ring for Governor. He was definitely under the thumb of the FBI director, J. Edgar Hoover. Nothing happened in Tampa that went unnoticed by this government agency. Cover–ups took place all the time. The cover–ups ranged from illegal whiskey and prostitution, to crimes on the high seas. This meeting was in regard to the latter. Guns were being smuggled into Cuba, in return for cigars and dope that were sold on the black market for a huge profit.

Bob Margolis was Hoover's man in Tampa and whatever went on was reported to the Director immediately. Hoover allowed Margolis and his friends a free hand in these trivial matters so he could use them for his personal vendettas when need be.

Margolis sent his flunky to make a phone call. No sooner did he sit back down than Jock came in to haul Irene out! She was angry to say the least! As they got in the car she looked across the street, there under the streetlight was Curly. Jock put her in the backseat and drove off. Curly crossed the street and entered the bar, as she watched from the back window. "Sorry, Irene, duty called," Jock said. "Yeah, one of Margolis's boys called and you came running! You better be glad I like you, Jock. Most women would find your tactics rubbing them the wrong way!" "Now Irene, when have I rubbed you at all?" he said looking at her in a teasing way from the rearview mirror. "Never Jock. You know better. That's how I tolerate you! That and the fact that you're always willing to keep Jackie when I call you!" they laughed. He got out and opened the door from the outside, because there were no handles in the back of his car for transporting prisoners, and because he was a gentleman. Irene thanked him, and she went inside.

Just seeing Curly standing under that light made her ache. She checked on her sleeping four year old, marveling at how much she favored her father, then tried to sleep. Sleep was a luxury Irene rarely had. Her mind drifted back to her thirteenth birthday party. She smiled as she realized seeing him still had the same affect on her. She rubbed her arms as the chills waved across them. How could she still have those feelings after all he had put her through? Why couldn't she hate him? Every time she thought she did hate him, he showed up and the feelings stirred inside her like a hurricane in the gulf. She was doomed to a life of unrequited love and she knew it.

The mob had their fingers in many pies. Practically all sports were infiltrated with mob interest. Their interest in the dog tracks were strictly in concessions, but the sports with a human element, like baseball, football, or boxing were a different story. Many times players would take a dive or fall as a favor to a 'boss' or 'Don' as they were referred to. Hoover, as well as, Margolis was aware of the illegal betting that took place, but as with the gunrunning and other illegal activities, this went unchecked, too.

The entertainment business was certainly under the thumbs of the 'Families'. They showed no mercy for entertainers that refused their offers to help.

Around this time a young woman in the country music field came into the Saratoga. She was crying in her beer. "What's wrong, honey. Can I help you in some way?" Irene asked. "I'm all washed up...that's all," she continued to cry. "What do you mean?" Irene sat down across the booth. She recounted her sad story of how she had been a rising star, but was now in a slump and couldn't get a gig, much less a record deal. "I can't seem to get a song the labels will even listen to. I walk in the door and everyone goes to lunch!" she continued to cry until she passed out on the table.

When the bar closed the woman was still slumped over the table. Irene went over to her, shook her awake and asked if she could call her a cab. Laughing and with slurred speech, "Sure, honey I've been called worse!" Irene laughed, "No, I mean can I get you a ride?" "Oh, no...tanks, I have my car right out...there." She slurred and pointed. Irene knew she couldn't let her drive in this condition, so she put her sweater around her, gathered her things and had Mikey drive them to her house.

The next morning, Irene got up and cooked breakfast. Jackie came bounding into the living room and saw the lady on the couch. "Mama, who is she?" she asked looking right into the woman's face. "Shh...don't wake her." Irene said. Jackie put her forefinger up to her mouth and tiptoed to the table. The smell of food aroused the singer. She sat up on the couch, looked around in confusion, and then said, "Hey, how did I get here?" Irene was bent over looking in the refrigerator for the jelly as the woman spoke, then she turned to look at her, "Good morning, you hungry?" "Yeah, I am. Do you have anything stronger than coffee?" "Not here. I just have that at work. Go ahead and wash up, Jackie will show you where." "Well hello there sweetie, I'm Bonnie. What's your name?" Jackie took her hand, "I'm Jackie, but that's not my real name. My real name is Jacqueline." "That's a mighty pretty name, kind of long for a little bitty thing, though. I think Jackie fits you." Jackie stood by the door waiting to escort her to the table. She could hear her singing over the sound of the water. When she came out Jackie said, "You sing pretty like my Mama." "Your mama sings? "Uh–huh." she replied. "You're pretty like mama, too," she said.

Bonnie was an attractive, petite woman with dark hair and eyes. She had the look of a star and the voice to match. When they got to the table Jackie said, "Mama, Bonnie sings pretty songs like yours." "Really? You said something last night about singing. I thought it was a dream coming through the alcohol." "No, it used to be a dream, then it was reality, and now it's dead! I had a good career going on for awhile. I just never could get that one song that could get me over the top. Big songwriters don't want to take chances on a newcomer. If I had been lucky enough to have that first real hit they would have begged me to record their stuff!" Irene set her plate on the table as she continued. "You know how it is, when you can't work at what you want you have to do things you would never dream of just to survive. I got mixed up with Eddie, this gopher for Trafficante, and he thought he owned me. He used me for transportation of goods, if you know what I mean?" Irene wasn't sure she did know, but she could imagine. "Anyway, they made me an offer I had to refuse and I just got out of the hospital a few days ago. Anyway, I'm heading back to Nashville. I've got to find that one big hit, you know?" She began wolfing her food down as Irene said, "I write lyrics, I sing the tunes, can't write music. My husband took some of my songs to Nashville and somebody recorded them. I never got anything out of it, not even recognition." "Ouch, that was a tough break! What kind of explanation did you get for that one?" "Oh, it's a long story. Tell you what, I'll write the lyrics if you write the music." Irene offered. "How long will you be in town?" "Not long, I've got to find something to do to make gas money out of here. I need to get out as soon as possible, you know, because of Eddie," she replied. "Where are you staying?" "In my car. It's not much, but it's home!" she said with a smile. "Tell you what, you stay here and help me out with Jackie and cleaning up and stuff, we'll write a couple of songs and I'll see you get gas money and a little extra for food. How does that sound?" Jackie began jumping up and down, "Please, Bonnie! Please stay, Please!" "Well, I have had offers lately that were not too good to refuse, this one would be! You've got your-self a housemate! Let me just go out to the car and get my guitar," she said. as she got up from the table. "You came home with me last night, you were in no condition to drive your car, its still at the Saratoga. You can get it after while. You can use my mother's room. She left this morning to visit my sister in Georgia for a couple of weeks. She usually watches Jackie while I work, so you see, you'll be helping me out too."

As they cleaned the house and washed the dishes, Bonnie hummed and Irene made up words to go with it. Jackie played 'air' guitar! They all seemed to be enjoying themselves. When it was time for Irene to go to work, they all went. Bonnie took Jackie back to the house in her car.

When it was Jackie's bedtime, Bonnie sang and played her guitar softly. "Bonnie Guitar, Bonnie Guitar, I'm gonna call you that from now on!" Jackie proclaimed. "I like that name!" she replied. She continued to play until Jackie fell asleep. She was still playing when Irene came in. "Sounds good," she remarked. "Yeah, it is kind of pretty. Can you write pretty words to it?" "I'll try, I do my best work when I first get up, while I'm hav-ing my coffee. In the morning after breakfast I'll write while you play." "That's a deal."

For nearly two weeks Bonnie and Irene spent every spare moment working on their music. "Well, I guess I better get going. I think we have a couple of winners here, Irene. We need a contract, she said as she grabbed a napkin, scrawling a rustic contract and signing her name. Maybe this time you'll get credit for your hard work!" she said as she hugged Irene. "Take care of yourself, Bonnie, and stay off the booze, ok?" she whispered. "Come here little bitty Jackie! If you had your ears pierced, I'd give you my gold earrings, but since you don't, if you ever need me, just send me a message and tell me to send you my earrings. I'll come running. You listen for records from 'Bonnie Guitar', sweetie!" she hugged her and left. Irene never heard from 'Bonnie Guitar' or her songs again.

The 'families' had to maintain a certain respect, especially from their own. Cal was one of theirs, but occasionally he would work a scam like scalping tickets at a big game or touting at the dog track. Touting was a con where eight different people are given one of the numbers of the dogs in that race. They are told the number they are given will win the race. Marks pay big money for that tip. One of them has to win because there are only eight dogs in the race. This can go on until someone gets wise to it, and then all hell breaks loose! Cal did not make a habit of these little cons, because he knew he had to keep his nose clean. However, he loved a good con every now and then and would take the risk!

The 'Dons' became very upset if one of their own was arrested for stupidity and embarrassed them. Trafficante was not happy when Cal got a wild hair and was caught touting at the dog track, therefore he pulled no strings to keep him from serving a three year sentence in Raiford Prison. Cal would be forgiven for his little sin once he was out of prison and Trafficante found some way for him to make amends.

Irene received a letter from Cal asking her to take care of his 'friend', Billy, until he got out of jail. He told her he was a good person and had been railroaded because of his sexual preference, that and passing bad checks. He also told her he loved him. Although Irene did not understand this kind of relationship she knew if it were not any different to how she felt about Curly, she would help him. She thought about this being a good time to pay him back for beating Curly up, and being one of the causes of the annulment, and anything else he might have done she didn't know about! She couldn't do that however, she was too good a person and after all he was her family. She agreed for Billy to come stay with her until Cal's release.

Irene didn't have any real girlfriends she associated with outside the Saratoga. Most of the ladies she knew were of the 'evening' variety, and although they were kind and most had hearts of gold, she did not consider them good role models for Jackie. Unaware her brother Gus had been molesting Jackie since she was four, Irene would probably have considered some of those women better role models than Gus! Had Curly known about this sick perverted act being inflicted on his daughter, he would have killed him. Gus knew it, but it didn't stop him.

When Billy arrived, he was nothing like Irene had imagined. He looked taller than his five foot nine inches because he was so thin. His natural blonde hair was the color many women would 'dye' for. His sparkling blue eyes accented his almost chiseled facial features, and his mouth was just too pretty to be on a man! Billy would be considered 'sissy' by women and 'queer' by men with his prissy gait and speech. Billy became the best 'girl-friend' Irene 'never' had. She found she could talk to him about anything; of course she didn't, because some things would cause Cal to kill Curly when he got out.

Billy was good to Jackie and Mrs. Scott; he took care of all the chores, including the cooking and clothes washing, (which Irene hated since her wringer washer ordeal). Billy
became 'Uncle Billy' to Jackie; he was now part of the family.

Irene hadn't seen Curly in such a long time; she was lonely and missed the relationship they once had. Men at the bar frequently asked her out, but she wasn't sure going out with them was a good idea, since romance with any other man held no interest for her. However, she saw no harm in establishing a friendship with a member of the opposite sex, someone to take her to the movies or out to eat. She thought of Joe, how he had befriended her during her pregnancy. She hadn't heard from him in years, not since the time he came to the cabin and gave her the information she needed to rescue Jackie. She worried he had been found out for helping her.

Fred Anderson had become a frequent patron of the Saratoga, and had been asking Irene out. She had always turned him down for fear he may expect more than she was willing to give. Jock had seen her talking to the tall, burly, blonde Anderson in the bar one night and after her shift offered her a ride home, "Irene, that Anderson fellow is no good. You really need to watch him; he's a strong arm out of New Orleans. In fact, I've heard he just got back from Texas where he strong armed the owner of a bar there, one of Marcello's boys named Ruby." "Ruby? That's an odd name for a man! Besides he just asked me out to eat, Jock." I know it's none of my business, but you really do need to be careful." "I'll be careful, Jock. He's asked me out a couple of times, but I said no…until tonight. He's taking me to dinner tomorrow night," she said coyly. "Well, you had better be careful, that's all. What do you think Curly will say about this?" "Look Jock, I'm only having dinner with the guy, we're not plotting to kidnap the queen, or anything! Besides, Curly who?" she teased. "You know Curly who! You better be careful, Irene. You're playing a game that could have a very sore loser!" "Thanks for the tip, Jock. Really, I appreciate your concern. I don't mean to sound like I don't. I just get hungry for steak and companionship every once in a while. That's all…I promise." He got out of the car and opened the door for her. As she was going up the steps he said, "Don't be surprised if you see me tomorrow night while your out with Anderson, I just don't trust that guy." "Thanks Jock! I didn't know Mama had three sons! Goodnight big brother."

She kept her date with Fred. He was a perfect gentleman; he didn't even try to kiss her. She was glad he understood she wasn't interested in him in that way, and apparently he wasn't in her in that way either. Jock strolled through the restaurant a couple of times, but she ignored his presence. She hoped Fred didn't notice he was there.

They continued to go out on occasion and it was always the same, just friends. Irene was still naïve where men were concerned and didn't realize a man like Fred was a wolf in friends clothing! The next time they went out he tried to kiss her, she pushed him away saying, "NO!", he complied with her wishes, but she didn't realize someone like Fred would only take 'No' for an answer so many times.

She had never seen Fred's temper, nor had she seen him drunk, one night she saw both! They had eaten out and he had one too many. He wasn't staggering, but he was not himself. When they got to the car he began pawing her, she pulled away. He grabbed her, held her wrists as tight as he could and tried to kiss her. She turned her head, he held her wrists with one hand and with the other he snatched her face around and kissed her in the mouth! The whiskey taste of his kiss scared her; she freed her right hand and slapped him as hard as she could! He hit her back and didn't stop until he had knocked her out! He carried her home and left her on the porch. Billy found her the next morning, carried her inside, and took care of her.

This was a time of depression for Irene. The next few weeks proved to be very trying times. Her mother became ill, her ninety–seven year old aunt was dying in a nursing home, Cal was still in prison, Curly was not around and she felt in her heart his love for her was dead. She became very angry and decided to take charge of her life. Her first take–charge act was not allowing her aunt to die! She refused to loose anyone else she loved! She, Gus, and Billy went to the nursing home and brought Aunt Molly home with them! With Billy's help she nursed Aunt Molly and her mother back to health. She even taught Aunt Molly how to crochet again, something she loved, but had been unable to do since her stroke.

Aunt Molly and 'Granny', as Irene's Mother had become to everyone since Jackie could talk, was great company for the soon to be six year old. They played games with her, taught her Bible verses and her ABC's. Jackie would color and Aunt Molly would pretend to pay her using toilet paper! Jackie believed she was rich!

Irene hadn't heard from Fred in a while and figured he was laying low because of what he had done to her. One night, about a month later however, he came in the bar trying to apologize for his drunken behavior, but she wasn't interested in him or his apologies. She took his drink order without conversation. Then as she sat his drink on the bar, he grabbed her hand, "Damn it, I said I was sorry!" Jerking her hand from him she replied, "Yeah, we all know you're 'sorry'! Now leave me alone!" Mikey walked up and told Fred to go home, "You've had enough to drink. Don't come around here anymore Anderson, you're not welcomed." Fred reluctantly got down from his stool, slammed a twenty–dollar bill down on the bar and said to Irene, "You've started a fire in me woman, and I won't stop 'till I'm all burnt up!" She looked at him, and then dashed his last drink order in his face! He walked away, when he reached the door, he took out a match and lit it, holding it out where she could see it. Laughing, he blew it out and stumbled out the door. Mikey shook his head, "Don't worry about that jerk, Irene. He won't be back in here. He knows I have connections." Irene kissed Mikey on the forehead as she would her father, "Thanks Mikey. I don't know what I'd do without you." He smiled and said, "Its closing time, let me take you home." She was glad he had offered, she was a little uneasy about Fred.

"Mama tell me about Uncle Cal again." "Now, Jackie! It's time for school. You just remember what I told you about the thick glasses! If he gets here in time, I'll send him to get you after school."

School dismissed and as Jackie ran down the steps she heard someone calling her name. There behind the fence was a tall, larger figured, scruffy looking man with black–rimmed glasses waving at her. She recognized him from her mama's description; it was Uncle Cal! He had borrowed Gus's old station wagon and had parked across the street. She couldn't believe how large his hand felt wrapped around hers as she felt for her mama's ring. "Yeah, I brought the damn thing! You don't think I'd let some son of bitch snatch you again, do you?" he said chuckling. She squeezed his hand laughing, too.

When Irene got home they sat down to a meal Uncle Billy had spent all day preparing to celebrate Cal's homecoming.

Irene was glad to have Cal home, she felt safer knowing he would be just around the corner. Gus had moved to an apartment around the corner when Aunt Molly moved in. He found an apartment on his block for Billy and Cal, as well. Billy had promised to come everyday and take care of 'his ladies', as he referred to them. Irene was glad to have her family together again…all but one of them. The only one missing was in her heart, but she stilled yearned for his presence.

One night when it was slow at the Saratoga, Irene came home early to find her old friend Joe, waiting for her on the steps. Jackie didn't remember ever seeing him, but he kept telling her he knew her. He even teased her about having changed her diapers! He rolled up the sleeve of his left are revealing a tattoo, "Do you know what this says?" Jackie aq squinted her yes squinted looking closely she said, "Yeah, that's my name!" She crawled up in his lap and touched each letter as she spelled aloud, "J.A.C.Q.U.E.L.I.N.E , why do you have my name on your arm? Will it wash off?" He laughed, "No, it won't wash off. That was my little girl's name." "Are you my daddy?" she asked confused, but excitedly. Irene yelled from the bedroom, "Joe, what are you telling that child? You had better behave. He's your Uncle, Jackie." Tickling Jackie, and laughing he said, "Jacqueline was my little girl's name;" the laughter subsided as he bowed his head, "She's dead now, he said sadly. Jackie felt sorry for him and hugged him, "Don't be sad, Uncle Joe, it'll be all right." Before he could speak Irene came in, "Give Uncle Joe a great big kiss, it's your bedtime young lady." "Wait Mama, I wan to tell Uncle Joe about riding Shelia in the Gasporilla Parade!" "Well, all right, but make it quick." "Have you ever seen a real elephant, Uncle Joe?" He nodded. "I rode a real elephant in the Gasporilla Parade! Her name was Shelia and she came from India! Have you ever been to India, Uncle Joe?" "No, I'm afraid not," he said smiling. "Did you know I was a princess?" "Yeah, I thought I knew that," he said in jest. "I really was, but it was just for the parade." she said as she hugged him goodnight. "Come to bed Jackie." "I'm coming Mama."

"Goodnight, Princess Jacqueline," Joe mused. She curtsied awkwardly, then ran to her room.

Jackie asked Irene about Joe's little girl while she was being tucked in. She told her she was killed when she was four years old, and that she was named for her. Jackie cried. She didn't really understand death, but she knew it was permanent, and it made her sad that Uncle Joe would never see his little girl again. She cried until she went to sleep.

Joe didn't stay long. He told Irene he was in town on 'Family' business town on 'family business'. "Where's your big 'brother'?" she asked half mocking. "He's in D.C., I think. He'll be in Tampa in a few days or so, though." They hugged as he left. "You had better come by here before you leave." Irene commanded. "I see you tomorrow."

When Joe was out of sight Irene called Jock to tell him she knew Curly was due back in town, and if it were all the same to him she'd just as soon not be thrown into the slammer this time! She promised to stay out of the way. Jock laughed and told her she was overreacting. She laughed as she told him she might be, but her daughter needed her at home! He agreed and told her he would do what he could.

The next day Joe came by and asked if they would like to go with him to the Larry Park Zoo. Jackie loved the idea! Her favorite thing at the zoo was the Sky King airplane! It thrilled her when Joe held her up to sign her name in the airplane like the other kids. Jackie didn't want the day to end, but when it did she hugged her Uncle Joe and made him promise he would come back soon and take her to the zoo again. He promised and she went to sleep.

Irene was hoping she would see Curly when he was in town this time. She had heard from some of the regulars at the bar that he had been in town a couple of times. She wondered why he hadn't tried to contact her or at least come in the Saratoga. A couple of months ago he had given Mikey a hundred dollar bill for Irene. He told him to tell her to, "Buy the kid some decent school clothes." Which she did, happily. Jackie was happy about it, too. Irene had not told her they were from him It was just too hard to explain. She had decided to answer only what Jackie asked about her father, as she asked it, that's all she knew to do.

On Saturday afternoon Irene sent Cal to the market, Jackie went with him. He had gotten an old green pick-up truck from somewhere; it didn't look like much, but it ran good. As they headed down the Twenty Second Street Causeway, blacks were out and about as was their custom on Saturdays, in the South. Racial riots had been going on as the blacks fought for their Civil Rights. Today they were not rioting, however, they were shopping, minding their own business of the day –to- day living. Cal said, "Damn niggers everywhere you look these days! Jackie when I tell you, get in the floor!" They were stopped at a traffic light; just ahead on the left was a black man standing by himself smoking a cigarette. There were no other cars around them. Cal rolled his window down and reached under his seat pulling out a large gun! As he drove through the light he held the gun out the window and fired! In a playful voice he yelled, "Pow, Pow!" He was laughing. As Jackie crawled back up on the seat she saw through the back window the blood, the black man falling to his death, and other black men racing to the scene. She was too afraid to ask questions. Cal noticing the fright on her face remarked, "Ole Uncle Cal was just playin', Jackie. Don't you go worrying about that old Uncle Tom! And don't you tell anybody about this either. Understand?" She shook her head. She never told a soul...until now.

CHAPTER SEVEN

That night at the Saratoga, Fred made another appearance. He wanted Irene to give him another chance, bringing her flowers and candy, trying to be a real gentleman, but he still couldn't convince her to change her mind. "Come on, Irene. Now damn it, I've bought you these pretty flowers and sweet candy. Come on be sweet to me!" She just looked at him in disgust and shook her head. She walked off to wait on other customers; being Saturday night, the bar was crowded. When he realized she wasn't going to change her mind, he snatched up the flowers and candy and the first table he came to where a couple was sitting, he threw the flowers on the table, "Here, your old man wants you to have these!" He stormed out the door.

Irene knew Fred was mad when he left, so after closing she asked Mikey to take her home. They went by to ask Gus to sleep over at Irene's for safety. He slept on the livingroom floor. Irene felt better just knowing he was there.

When Gus had made sure everyone was asleep, he crept into Jackie's room and had his sick perverted way with her. Holding his hand over her mouth, he told her if she screamed or told anyone what 'they' were doing, she would get in trouble and so would her mother. He said she would be kidnapped from her mother, never to see her again. She cried silent tears as always during and after. About 4:00a.m. Jackie got out of bed to go to the bathroom. From the window, she saw flames flickering and sparks flying. Being in the state of mind she was in, she thought she was dreaming. As she walked back to her room Granny yelled, "Jackie, what is that smell, what's burning?" "It's nothing Granny, just the house burning," she answered in a sleepy voice. Granny began yelling for Gus and Irene.

Immediately Irene sent Jackie around the corner for Cal and Billy. She ran as fast as she could, but by the time they got back to the house, it was engulfed in flames! Irene and Gus had gotten Granny out safely and were in the house getting Aunt Molly. Cal ran in trying to save anything he could, but was overtaken by the smoke and had to leave empty handed.

The next day Irene, Cal and Gus carried Aunt Molly back to the nursing home, planning to leave her just until they found another house, but the smoke and excitement had been too much for her and she suffered another stroke. She died a few days later.

Irene, Jackie, and Granny moved to Corrine Street after the fire where they would remain for the next three years.

Cal had been asking questions about, "That damn Fred, bastard that had been bothering" Irene. She told him all that had happened, and that she wasn't ever having anything else to do with him. She said she had no control over who came in the bar. He said in a strong voice, "Yeah, well I can tell you one damn thing for sure, he don't want what I've got for him! He damn well better leave you alone!" Irene hugged her big brother and thanked him for wanting to fight her bully!

Jock told Irene, "The word on the street is the fire was mob connected, but the boys at the station don't think so. Anyway, Irene they won't take any chances, so don't look for them to do anything about it."

According to Mikey, Fred had been in the bar earlier that day bragging about having "burned the bitch's house down around her!" Cal was in the bar and overheard him. Fred, not knowing who Cal was, left with him to go find a couple of women! A few days later, Fred's beaten and partially burned body was found in his car, which was parked in front of the burned house!

About this time too, Cal was arrested for assault and robbery, a crime he may or may not have committed, and for which he was found innocent. Jock believed he was responsible for Fred's death, but Cal had an alibi for that night, Uncle Billy. At any rate, Cal had broken his last parole and received six months in jail.

Irene was feeling low because of Cal's incarceration, the fire, Aunt Molly's death, and not having seen Curly. It seemed everything was going wrong! One afternoon as she was getting ready for work a note was shoved under the door, *'Back stairs, 2:00a.m. Love C.'* Irene was so happy she began singing and twirling around the room. Jackie came in, picked up the note and read it aloud. "Hey, Mama, I remember when you got a note like this before!" Irene danced over to her and playfully snatched the note, tucking it into her blouse, "You sure are a nosey little thing! Who taught you to be so nosey?" She began tickling her and they fell on the bed, laughing Jackie replied, "Granny! Granny taught me!" They both laughed and laughed. "Scoot little nosey and let me get a shower and dress! It's your bedtime. I'll see you before I leave." "Ok, Mama. I'll stay awake 'til you come in." Irene did as she promised and went in to see Jackie just before leaving for the Saratoga. "Oh, Mama! You look so pretty! Will I be as pretty as you when I get grown?" "No, baby, you'll be much prettier! I'll be so jealous!" she hugged and kissed Jackie goodnight and left.

Her shift seemed longer than usual, but at the appointed time she walked out back to meet Curly on the stairs. They embraced under the stars and he kissed her. As usual she was under his spell! He invited her upstairs for a drink and late night dinner. He phoned the Chinese restaurant and placed his order, then sat on the couch beside her and said, "How have you been, Irene?" "I've been better, Curly. How about you?" she replied. "I've been hearing about you dating, Irene and you know you shouldn't be doing that. You're wearing my brand, Babe. That means you belong to me." He said matter of factly. "Oh, really? I didn't realize you still cared. I don't see you enough to give you exclusive rights," she quipped. He grabbed and kissed her, then held her head back with his hands meshed in her hair, "I'm not kidding, Irene! Don't play with me like that. You're mine and I'll kill any son of a bitch that messes with you!" "Ok…Curly but, nothing happened with that guy! You know you're the only man I've ever…" "Shut up Irene, and kiss me," he whispered. Just as they were heating up a knock came at the door. Curly rearranging his clothes went to the door, returning with several cartons of Chinese food. "The perfect food depicting our relationship, 'Sweet and Sour'!" He laughed; she tried to laugh, but didn't see the humor. Before she finished her meal she became emotional and ran into the bathroom, locking the door. He ran after her, giggling the doorknob to get in, "Irene, what's wrong? Let me in Irene, what's wrong?" "Leave me alone Curly!" she cried. "Open the damn door, Irene! I mean it, damn it, open the fucking door!" When she didn't answer, he kicked the door open, "You should know there's not a fucking door or man or anything that will keep me out, Irene! Now what the hell is wrong with you?" he demanded sitting in the floor beside her. "You! You're the matter with me! You've been the matter with me since I was thirteen years old! You stay gone all the time, you never try to see Jackie, and you want to know what's the matter with me?" "Irene, you know why I can't be here. It's not safe for Jackie." "But you are missing so much of her life, Curly! She needs her father!" Putting his arms around her he whispers, "Tell me about her, Irene. I need her, too." "She's wonderful, Curly! She is so smart and cute! She dresses up in my old clothes and puts make–up on pretending to be a movie star." "Oh, hell! I hope she won't go there!" they laughed. "Come on, let's get out of the floor." He gently helped her to the bed where he took her in his arms, "God, I love you, Irene! I miss you; I miss us. I wish we could be a family like Ozzie and Harriet! Damn my family!" Irene tried to console him. She kissed him, they engaged in breathless sex melting in each other and becoming one as they should be.

Later, Curly excused himself to fix them a drink. Although she tended bar, she had never let hard liquor pass her lips. Curly talked her into having a glass of his scotch, it burned and reminded her of Fred's mouth the night he kissed her! She didn't really want it, but it appeared to be amusing him, so she killed it! A few minutes later she was so sleepy she couldn't make herself stay awake.

When she awoke the next morning, she was alone. A single yellow rose lay on the pillow beside her. She lay with mixed emotions, satisfied womanly, but empty otherwise. As she rolled out of bed she felt the familiar pain across her breasts, she began to moan with the thought of the wringer washing machine incident. She slowly raised the sheet and peered at her breasts. She saw writing on both, but the redness and bruising made it hard to make out the words. She wrapped up in the sheet and went to the mirror where she slowly read the words that appeared backward, 'Sweet' on the right breast, and 'Sour' on the left. As she read the words, she remembered their conversation and drinks last evening. The thought behind this ritual was a pleasant memory, and she wasn't going to let this new 'branding' ruin those memories. In fact, she rather liked being his branded woman. As she turned to get dressed she grabbed her shoulder, it felt as if something had stung her. She found the tiny numbers forty–seven through fifty–nine scrolled across her arm! She recognized most of the numbers as years of their romance, but didn't know the meaning of some. She decided not to care, she knew he would tell her someday, if it were important for her to know. As she started to leave, she found a book of matches, 'Sailor Sam Tattoo Artist' and the phone number. Also there was a hundred dollar bill under the ashtray. She left the flat…empty and alone.

Several months passed, Irene was working from three to close. The hours were longer, but the tips were good. Small's shrimp crews coming and going made business boom.

Jock told Irene that Curly was back in town on 'family' business. She asked him to give Curly a message for her; she needed to see him. He told her he couldn't make any promises, but he would try.

The next day a note was sent to the bar, *'3:00a.m. stairs, C'.* Irene had made up her mind to confront the situation head on. She wanted to know when he planned to take some responsibility for his child. She was getting older and required more than milk and diapers! She had gone along with his non–participation in Jackie's life, but believed in her heart that he would change his mind about his 'family's' right to dictate his involvement in their lives.

When she saw him, the same emotions that she had always had for him came rushing back, but somehow, she bridled her emotions and stood her ground. When he reached for her hand she didn't extend it, she looked him in the eyes as she said, "Thanks for coming. We need to talk." The look on his face was worth a million dollars! For once she could see through to his soul! No pretense as she said, "I have been working twelve and fourteen hours a day to make a living for your daughter, Curly. Don't you think it's about time you stop letting your 'family' dictate how much and when you participate in her life? She's growing up and needs clothes and things for school. How can you just allow her to do without?" The entire time she spoke, he looked directly into her eyes with no emotion. When she had finished he said, "Can we go inside now?" Irene couldn't believe she had stood outside on the stairs and said all this to him! She spoke not another word until they got inside, "Curly you know I'm right. Jacqueline is already beginning to ask questions about you. She asks Mama because she doesn't want to upset me. It's not fair to her to be without her father, Curly. It would be different if her father was dead, but he is very much alive and that's wrong, Curly and you know it!" her words burned his ears, he snapped, "You were told to leave well enough alone when I had her, but you just couldn't do it! Now, you understand what was meant when you were told she would have a better life! I'm doing the best I can, if you want more, that's too damn bad. I can't be here and there and everywhere. I'm sorry." She couldn't believe what she was hearing! Was he actually admitting to kidnapping Jackie? "I can't help what kind of obligations you think you have to your 'family', Curly, but she's your family, too! I know I love you more than they ever could, and Jackie…" He grabbed her and kissed her before she could finish, then he stopped. Every time she would open her mouth to speak he kissed her again. This cat and mouse game continued until their sexual urges were over powering and before they knew what was happening, they were completely naked and totally engulfed in each other. When their passion had been quenched they lay in silence for a long time. Finally, he spoke, "I told you before, I was not consulted about the annulment. I had no choice in the matter then, and I have no choice now. It's not that I don't love you and Jacqueline, I do." She interrupted, "But you can't do anything unless they allow you to. That excuse is getting a little old, Curly. You really need to come up with a better one." He lit a cigarette, "You need to keep your mouth shut, Irene about things you know nothing about. It's no time for you to start anything. You're insignificant in the grand scheme of things that are happening now. You're a peon, a nothing, like me. The world as we know it is about to change. History is about to have another chapter ripped from its pages, and our wants and needs are the last things on anybody's agenda right now. You had better just settle down and go with the flow." As he spoke his riddles, she began dressing. For the first time, she would leave him in the afterglow. Without another word, she walked out the door and down the stairs. She didn't even look back.

The next day, Gus left on a shrimp boat to New Orleans and according to Mikey, Curly was on the same boat. Curly left an envelope for Irene containing five hundred dollars and a note, *'More later. There's a present for Jacqueline at Gus's house. Love you both, C.'* Irene put the money in her bra and tore the note up, put it in the ashtray and watched without expression as it burned. She still loved him, but something stirred an eerie feeling in her soul. A feeling of dread, she couldn't escape. The feeling she had when she found out their marriage no longer existed was about equal in horror to this!

On the way home, she stopped by Gus's to get Jackie's present. Billy had the key and let her in. She told him she wouldn't be but a minute she had left something there the other night when she was over. She couldn't mention Curly and Gus to Cal it was too dangerous, and Billy might say something. Billy said he was just leaving and would see her later. She went in to find an orange dress with flowers and ruffles. She cried when she saw it, she knew he had chosen it himself and she wished she could tell Jackie where it came from…she couldn't.

When she got home, she gave the dress to Jackie. She was so excited, she put it on and modeled it, swirling and twirling. She hugged Irene and thanked her as if she had given her the dress. Irene hugged her back and whispered, "I'll tell him you loved it." "What? What did you say Mama?" "Just that you look beautiful, Baby."

About a week later Curly and Gus returned. Something was definitely going on because Mikey was nervous. "What's going on, Mikey? What's got you so agitated?" "Irene, you need to take off tomorrow night. I'll pay you your regular hours and give you extra for the tips you'll miss." "Why? What's up?" "You know I can't discuss that, Irene. Just take my word for it and stay home!" "Ok, Jackie will love having me home two nights in a row." As she lay in bed the next night, she could think of nothing but what was going on at the Saratoga and what Curly and Gus had to do with it.

"More drinks over here Mikey!" a voice called over the noise. Mikey obliged. Suddenly, a hush fell over the bar as Santos Trafficante, Carlos Marcello, and representing the Patrillo family, Curly, walked into the bar and sat together at the same table. Cal put his hand on a chair and lifted it slightly off the floor, looking at Curly as if he were going to ram him with it. "Put the chair down. We have organization business here tonight, boys. 'One, big, happy family'. Everyone place your piece on the table in plain sight, and those not carrying, sit down," Trafficante ordered. Cal sat down, as did several others. Talk went on at the main table and the 'suits' kept drinking quietly. Soon Marcello stood, "Boys, we're uniting for the good of 'family' and country. Until further word there will be a truce among the organizations. Each of you will be given your assignment in the usual manner. Goodnight." When the 'suits' had left, Marcello told Curly, "Sam G. is meeting with Edgar as we speak. Sammy will meet you boys in New Orleans. You know what to do from there."

CHAPTER EIGHT

It was no secret there was no love lost between J. Edgar Hoover and the Kennedy's. Nothing would have made Hoover happier than for John Kennedy to serve only four years or less of his present term. Kennedy, on the other hand had higher aspirations, he intended to serve two terms.

Kennedy knew in order to gain re–election, he would have to narrow the gap and develop better relations with minority groups, as well as, labor relations. He was also aware of the Cuban contraband that had been taking place involving the Trafficante, Marcello, and Patrillo families. He had gotten word that the families had joined forces in an effort to assassinate Fidel Castro.

Because of the Bay of Pigs incident, Kennedy wasn't interested in any more bad Cuban publicity.

En route to Dallas, Kennedy scheduled a meeting with the Labor Union in Tampa as well as, the Latino community to help gain their support in the upcoming election. That same day, he made an unscheduled stop to Corrine Street to gain information about the mob plot to kill Castro.

It was time for school to dismiss and Jackie skipped the entire block home. When she reached her house, a big black car with dark windows was parked in the yard. Two men dressed in black suits, hats, and sunglasses were standing by the car. Jackie slowly approached and made her way up the steps to the porch where Granny was sitting in her green wicker rocker talking to a tall, bushy headed man with kind eyes and a toothy smile. Granny smiled and asked if she knew who the man was, "No ma'am," she replied. The man smiled, took a seat next to Granny and motioned for Jackie to come to him. He put his arm around her waist as

Granny said, "This is President John F. Kennedy, Jacqueline." The President remarked, "Jacqueline is my wife's name, and I have a little girl, too. What grade are you in, Jackie? About the second I would guess." "Yes sir, I'm in the second grade. How did you know that?" she asked. "I'm a good guesser, Jackie!" he laughed. Granny told her to go inside and change her school clothes. She went inside as she was told, but by the time she returned to the porch, Granny was alone. She could see the red taillights of the big black car as it drove out of sight. She was disappointed that she didn't get to say goodbye, "Granny, why was the President at our house?" In her vague response she explained that he was asking for Uncle Cal." "Is Uncle Cal in trouble?" Jackie asked. "No, he just gets blamed for things he don't do," Granny replied.

When Irene came home, Granny was waiting up for her. When she came in, Jackie came running out of her bedroom, "What's going on around here you two?" she asked. Then Granny scolded Jackie for being up so late on a school night. "But, Granny, I couldn't sleep! I had to tell Mama about the President!" "What about him? Irene asked. "He came to see Granny today!" "What? Mama, what is she talking about?" Irene asked with confusion. "Jackie you need to go on to bed now, so your mama and I can talk...and don't tell anybody at school that he was here," Granny commanded. "Oh, all right! I'm going, I'm going!" Jackie replied disappointedly. "Scoot little one," Mama said as she playfully swatted her behind with her sweater, "I'll be there to tuck you in shortly." Jackie did as she was told...almost. She stopped at her doorway so she could hear what Granny was telling her Mama.

"Jackie was telling the truth about Kennedy, Irene. He was here this afternoon." "What in the world, Mama? Why would the President of the United States come here?" she asked. "Well, I thought he was here because of the letters I've been writing about Cal being sent to prison when he didn't do anything. Now I know he's not perfect mind you, but some of this just ain't right, Irene." "You've been writing letters, Mama? Who did you send them to?" "Well, let's see, I sent one to the Mayor, the Governor, and to him, President John F. Kennedy, but that wasn't why he was here, Irene. He wanted to know if Cal was here and who he worked for. I told him he did odd jobs on the shrimp boats and I thought he worked for Chet Small. Then he asked me if I had ever heard Cal mention Trafficante, Marcello, Patrillo, Glisson, or Hoover. I said I wasn't sure, maybe. Then I remembered your name was Glisson and Curly and I told him that. He wanted to know if Curly was here. I told him you' weren't together anymore on a regular basis, but I knew you said he had gone to New Orleans so I told him that." "Mama! I wish you hadn't told him any of that, especially about Curly. You know he doesn't want me to discuss his business with anyone." Irene was terribly upset. "Well, he makes me mad, Irene. You let him get by with too much! It's none of my business, but I wish you'd just let him go and forget about him!" "Mama, you know I can't do that. Please just leave things alone. Don't answer any more questions, please." "Well, you know I just worry about you that's all." "I know Mama, I know." Irene kissed her mother on the forehead and headed to tuck Jackie in. Jackie heard her coming and jumped in the bed, pulling the covers over her head, pretending to be fast asleep. She didn't want her mother to know she had heard part of what they were saying. As usual, Granny whispered on all the good parts!

The next day at school the teacher allowed the class to watch President Kennedy's trip to Dallas on television. Jackie was excited and was having a really hard time keeping his visit to herself. Then a shot rang out, the President slumped over, and the newscaster shouted, "He's been shot! The President has been shot!" Jackie jumped up and ran out of the room, down the hall, and home! She cried all the way.

Granny had the television on, she was crying, too. Soon the whole world would know the leader of the free world was dead. Irene came in from the grocery store where she had learned the news. She put the groceries away and went straight to her room, where in her mind she replayed her last conversation with Curly, and the conversation with her mother. She didn't want to think about either, but she just couldn't help herself.

She was afraid this was what Curly was talking about when he said the history books would be forever changed. Her horrible feeling was now replaced with sad uncertainty for herself and the rest of the country.

After Kennedy's death the Tampa authorities seemed more interested in Irene. Jock spent a lot more time at the Saratoga than before, Gus was out on the shrimp boats, and Curly wasn't around. Cal was in jail, again.

"Had any special guests at your house lately, Irene?" Jock asked. "No, Curly hasn't been around in a while," she replied. "I wasn't talking about Curly, Irene," he said. She just looked at him a minute then said, "Now Jock, why would you be asking me, you're the detective. I thought you knew every time somebody sneezes around here," she quipped. Jock snickered and shook his head as he left.

Since Cal was incarcerated the trumped up charges were being made against Irene. Several times she had been arrested for 'B–Drinking', which was a scam where the barmaid would allow a man to buy her a drink, but instead of liquor, she would drink tea, and charge the man the price of the alcoholic drink." She was also arrested for prostitution, was accused of 'rolling' customers on several occasions, and sometimes, just for aggravation she would be handcuffed and ridden around in an unmarked car where she would be questioned about her knowledge of Cal or Curly.

Most of the time she wasn't formally charged, but several times she was brought before the Judge. He warned her against having to be brought before him again. She remembered a judge telling Cal and Gus that, when he called them 'animals'! She felt like an animal and she wanted to tell the judge that being here was not her idea, the charges were bogus. Her court appointed attorney advised her against it. She wondered which 'family's' pocket her attorney and the judge were in, but thought better of asking. The judge dismissed her case.

Mikey told Irene he could only let her work a couple of weekdays. She asked, "If you have to cut back Mikey, I understand, but can't I at least work Friday and Saturday so I'll have the tips?" He shrugged his shoulders and said, "You know how it is around here, Irene." "Don't tell me they've gotten to you, too!" "Come on Irene, it won't be forever. Just let things set-tle down a little, that's all." "Yeah, well tell me this, Mikey, how am I going to feed my daughter and mother, much less keep a roof over our heads, huh? Do you think when they are hungry my telling them it won't be for-ever, let things settle down, will fill their bellies?" He didn't have an answer for her, so he handed her the last full paycheck she had coming. "I'm sorry, Irene. You know if I were not being leaned on, I wouldn't do this. It's a matter of survival." Nodding she replied, "Yeah, I know. I hope you sur-vive, Mikey. I really do. But, right now I have enough survival to worry about. I can't afford to add you to my list." With that she left.

She used her check to pay the rent and buy food that would be enough to last only a week. Granny's little check was enough for utilities. She did-n't know what she would do next. She went all over town looking for work, but nobody would hire her. Gus was still on the shrimp boats, Curly was who knew where, and Cal was in prison! Billy was staying with Irene again, he was good to Irene and her family, but when it came to working, he was useless! He had become part of the family and she couldn't turn him out to starve! She was scared. She had never felt so helpless or alone.

One morning after all the money was gone, she found a Welfare check belonging to a black woman living in the bottoms in the mailbox. She knew who the woman was and that three other people living in her house were also receiving checks. She wrestled with her conscience about keep-ing it and using the money to buy food and pay rent. She put it in her pocket while she pondered the situation. She went to the kitchen, Billy informed her, there was one package of pinto beans and that was it! She knew what she had to do. Survival won her conscience over. She told her-self, if she weren't sure that the woman and her children would not starve, she would not take the check. However, she knew in her heart the other people living with her wouldn't allow that to happen. She thought about getting Billy to take the check and cash it, but because he had already served time for cashing bad checks she didn't want to involve him.

The next day, she went to Tarpon Springs, a mostly Greek community, far enough away from Tampa so she would not know anyone, and bought a bill of groceries. The clerk took the check with no questions asked. She was nervous and felt terrible about what she had done. She promised herself that she would give the money back to it's rightful recipient just as soon as Gus or Curly showed up.

Less than a week went by and the money was dwindling. She was getting worried and knew if something didn't happen soon they would be evicted!

One afternoon, just after they had finished eating, Jock knocked on the door. He had an arrest warrant for Irene. "Irene, you've really done it this time! I can't help you out of this one. Stealing someone's government check is a federal offense. What on earth were you thinking? You'll have to come with me, I'm sorry." Bowing her head in shame, "Will you give me a minute to talk to Mama, please?" she asked softly. "Sure, go ahead, but don't be long, the Captain sent me and he'll be all over me."

Telling her mother was one of the hardest things she had ever done. She knew she couldn't explain to Jackie, so she just told her she had to go with Jock and would be back as soon as she could.

She was in jail overnight. The next morning she was arraigned, bail was set, and a trial date set for a month later. Jock told Mikey what had happened to Irene. He felt so responsible, he posted her bail and gave her enough money for food and rent. She went home to await trial.

Gus came home two weeks later. Irene was never so glad to see him. She told him what had happened and that he had better see to it the family was taken care of while she was away. Jock had warned her she would probably have to serve time. Gus promised her he would take care of things; she could count on it.

The Judge that heard Irene's case had a reputation for being an iron armed judge, nicknamed, 'Hangin' Harry'. The bailiff called, "All Rise!"

The Judge came in and slammed his gavel. Irene jumped, just as she had at Gus and Cal's trial. He looked over his glasses at her with disapproval. Starring at her with cold eyes he said, "You've been associating with some pretty shady characters, Missy. I'm afraid some of their bad habits have rubbed off on you. This is a very serious crime you have pleaded guilty to, a federal offense. Do you have anything you wish to say in your defense before I pronounce your sentence?" Irene began to speak, "I…" "Stand up, please." He reprimanded. As she stood she said, "I'm sorry for what I had to do your Honor. I only did it because my family would have gone hungry otherwise." She sat back down. "Mrs. Glisson you should have applied for welfare assistance yourself if your family was in such dire need. That is what it is there for! Stand please. Irene Scott Glisson you have pleaded guilty to the charges of stealing a federal check and forgery. It is therefore the judgment of this court that you shall receive a sentence based on that plea. In view of the fact you have no prior convictions, I sentence you to one year and one day in federal prison. Because I believe you would be best served by spending time away from your known criminal associates, I am transferring you to a federal women's prison in Virginia, where you will remain for the duration of your sentence. He pounded his gavel and yelled, "Court dismissed! Bailiff, take this woman into custody." Irene's knees felt weak as the authorities led her to her cell.

Jock brought Jackie to the jail and the Sheriff allowed Irene to see her in his office without handcuffs. Jock told Irene the Judge had written an order for Jackie to remain in the custody of her mother. She was relieved as she feared Jackie would be placed in foster care, and that scared her to death! When Irene saw Jackie she didn't know what to say. She didn't want her daughter to know she was going to jail. She told her she had to go away for awhile, but while she was away she would write as often as she could, but Jackie could write to her everyday. She hugged her little girl and kissed her over and over again. They said goodbye and Jock took Jackie home. Irene was put on a prison bus to Virginia. As it left she looked out the back window where she saw Curly leaning against his car in front of the jail. She watched until the bus turned the corner and he was out of sight.

CHAPTER NINE

Irene used her prison time for self– improvement. She studied, passed a two–year college equivalency test, and had dental work she had not been able to afford.

Through her letters, she and Jackie played hide and seek. In each letter she would have Jackie look for her in a different place. Irene thought the game would help pass the time for Jackie until she came home again.

Cal escaped from Raiford Prison by hijacking a truck and 'Kidnapping' the driver. The FBI was called in and headed for his mother's house.

Two FBI agents went to the school for Jackie. When she was taken to the office the Principal said, "Jacqueline, these gentlemen work for the United States government, and they have come to take you to your grandmother." Jackie looked puzzled and asked, "Did you bring me anything?" The agents looked at each other and then the principal, shrugging they answered in unison, "No, were we supposed to." Jackie asked if she could see the principal in the hallway. He obliged. "What's the matter Jacqueline?" "Mr. Bailey, I can't go with them." "Why not?" "They don't have my mama's ring. She said I was to never go with anybody that I didn't know if they didn't show me her ring when I asked if they brought me anything. I can't go with them." "Now Jacqueline, they have shown me their credentials and I know they are who they say, you must go with them." "No, sir. I won't! My mama said I can't! I was kidnapped once and mama is afraid. I can't go Mr. Bailey!" "Well," he said rubbing his head, "Let me speak with them." He did and they left. They came back with Mrs. Scott, and Jackie went home.

The FBI hid in the attic for four days awaiting Cal's arrival. Cal didn't come home until the sixth day! The driver pulled the truck into the yard. Cal and the driver went into the house and had breakfast with Granny and Jackie. 'That man doesn't look like he is here against his will like the news said', Granny thought. When he had finished eating his meal, the driver thanked Granny, shook hands with Cal, "Well, buddy I'll see you later." "Yeah, thanks for the ride." With that he left in the truck! About an hour later the FBI stormed through the front door to take Cal into custody. "Damn, man did you have to break my mama's fucking door? Didn't your mama teach you to knock? Damn!"

Mrs. Scott heard Cal's conversation and hobbling over to him hit him upside the head with her cane! "I've told you to watch you mouth, Cal. I mean it too!" Shaking her cane, "And as for you two, you can fix my door before you leave or I'll give you a lesson, too!" "We're sorry about your door ma'am, but we're not allowed to fix it." By this time she had gotten a hammer out from under the sink, "Well, then you'll have to wait for Cal to fix it. You can't leave an old woman and little girl here alone with an unlocked door." They waited for Cal.

He would serve out his current term with three months remaining, plus an extra six months for his little vacation.

When school was out for the summer, Granny sent Jackie to stay with an aunt and uncle in Hollywood, Florida. Aunt Alice and Uncle John owned a junk car yard, which they used to build stock cars. They raced the cars all over the south. Their best car was S44, driven by Cory Wolff. Wolff was racing at one of the Golden Gate tracks when he crashed and burned S44. Jackie was scared when she saw the car burning; it brought back memories of their house burning. She began to cry uncontrollably. Alice took her to the press box where special guest, Ronald Reagan was sitting. He was kind to Jackie, telling her jokes, talking about school, and letting her think she was using the microphone. He took Jackie to the hospital to her aunt and uncle, where he stayed until the doctor gave his report on Cory. The prognosis was good, although he was burned over seventy percent of his body, he would survive.

A couple of days later she saw Reagan again. She hugged him and thanked him for helping her. "That's what I'm here for, and if there is ever anything you need, just let me know," he said with a smile.

A few weeks later, she returned to Granny. She missed home and especially her mother; she did not miss Gus's late night visits and dreaded them. She was anxious to write her mother about meeting Ronald Reagan, Aunt Alice had told her he was a famous actor.

Back home she still missed Irene. Her fears about Gus were realized the night she got home. She was happy when Granny said he had to go to work on the shrimp boats. Billy was still staying with them and Jackie was glad of that, she wished she could tell somebody about Gus.

With the help of Granny she wrote Irene nearly everyday. Irene would answer with a clue to where she was and Jackie would search for her. One morning, as she sat down to eat breakfast, Granny was re–reading Irene's last letter, she gasped, "Jackie! You're going to find your mother at the front door!" Jackie jumped up from the table and dashed to the door, there was a big bus stopped across the street, in front of the neighborhood store, Ma Head's. As the bus pulled away from the curb, Irene was standing there! They ran meeting in the middle of the road, where they stood hugging and kissing until a car horn interrupted their reunion.

Billy had prepared breakfast, and they all sat down to eat. Jackie went to the refrigerator for juice, as she opened the door, the percolator fell, splattering hot coffee and grounds all over her! Irene jumped up to blot the spill from Jackie's body. Jackie was screaming to the top of her lungs. The milkman came to the door and heard the screaming, he knocked, but couldn't be heard, he stepped inside to see if he could be of assistance. He grabbed butter from the refrigerator and pushing Irene out of the way, began slathering Jackie with it. He told Irene to get his wallet out of his back pocket, take the ten dollars and get a taxi. He advised against waiting for an ambulance. She did as she was told. They wrapped Jackie in a sheet and headed to the hospital, where she would remain for a week with second and third degree burns.

Irene rested her head on the hospital bed as Jackie slept. A familiar touch on her arm caused her to jump. She looked up to see Curly standing there. He squeezed Jackie's blanket covered foot and whispered, "How's she doing?" Irene couldn't hold her tears back as she replied, "The doctors say she will be fine, the scars won't be too bad. They probably won't be noticeable; she has fair complexion like you," she answered softly. He walked around to the other side of the bed, bent down and kissed Jackie on the forehead, "Are you all right, Irene?" "Yeah, I'm ok. I'm just sick about this. I don't know how things happen so quickly!" "You can't dwell on things you can't do anything about, Irene. Shit happens, that's all." He walked back around to be closer to Irene. He sat on the edge of the bed holding Jackie's hand with his left hand and Irene's right. "I've missed you." He said as he squeezed her hand. She squeezed his hand, but made no comment. "She's gonna be all right, Irene. She has two stubborn parents and it's my guess she is, too. She won't let this keep her down. She'll be out playing in no time." "I guess you're right. I just can't stand to see her hurting." "I think you're in more pain than she is right now, she looks pretty happy to me!" They laughed quietly as Jackie snored. He stayed for over an hour. "I have to be going now. I just had to make sure my girls were all right." Irene had dropped her head when he said he had to go, he lifted her chin and kissed her, "I love you and my little girl," he declared. He walked to the door, turned to take one more look then, closed the door.

When Jackie was out of the hospital, Irene went back to work for Mikey. He gave her more hours and three hundred dollars Curly had left for her.

She had done a great deal of thinking while she was away, and decided that she had to let go of her past and take care of Jackie's future. However, she was in no position to turn down the money. She justified taking the money because he should be supporting his daughter. She told Mikey to keep the money for the bail he had paid, he said Curly had taken care of that as well. She took the money and kept her promise. She couldn't face the woman she had stolen from, but she got a money order and mailed it to her with a note of apology and explanation. She felt cleansed, absolved of her sin.

While in jail, Irene had been diagnosed with diabetes. She had to go to the free government clinic for her medication. There she met a woman named Edie Baker. Edie was a strikingly beautiful woman with raven hair and alabaster complexion, her eyes were almond shaped and black as coal. Edie lived just down the street, and after meeting Irene, became a frequent patron of the Saratoga. When Irene began working from two in the afternoon until two in the morning, she asked Edie to help Billy out with Granny and Jackie. Edie would cook dinner occasionally, run errands, or be there when Billy needed to get out. In turn, she would eat at least one good meal a day.

Irene had also met a man at the bar, Marvin Maxwell. He seemed nice and well to do. He tried to court her with little gifts, flowers, and candy, but she just wasn't interested in a romance. She had learned her lesson about thinking she could go out to dinner and just be friends. Fred Anderson had taught her that much! Mikey had told her he really didn't know anything about Anderson except that he had seen him with one of Marcello's boys a couple of times. When she found that out she told him she was not interested and refused his gifts and flowers. He, like Fred wouldn't take 'No' for an answer and began stalking her. She talked to Jock and he would come by at closing and take her home every night. When he left, Marvin would park in front of the house or stand across the street under the street lamp, just starring at her house. One morning after he had stood across the street, Irene counted eighteen cigarette butts, all the brand Marvin smoked! She knew he had stood there from the time Jock left until daylight! She was beginning to be afraid. She called Jock and asked to see him. She told him about Marvin being across the street until daylight, but Jock told her all he could do was see her safely home.

He said he couldn't arrest someone for smoking under a streetlight, and he admitted his captain would have his badge if he knew he was even escorting her home.

Irene talked to Gus about Marvin and he agreed to come stay at night for awhile. Jackie was not happy about that, and for good reason. Each night he slipped into her room and committed his horrible secret crime. She would beg Irene to let her sleep with her, finally she consented when Jackie told her she was scared of that man. Billy had a habit of staying up until Irene was safe at home and Gus would not attempt anything as long as someone was up. She hated for her mama to be afraid, but she was glad she had an excuse to get away from Gus!

Irene did not mention Marvin in her letters to Cal, for fear of what he might do when he got out. She knew he had more to do with Fred's death than he would admit.

The stalking continued. He came in the bar about six each evening and stayed until Irene got off. Mikey tried to tell him to leave, but he said as long as he was a paying customer and wasn't disturbing the peace he had a right to be there. Finally, Irene told Cal about Marvin and he told her to just keep doing what she was doing and he would eventually get tired and go away.

Cal was due home a week after Irene had received his response to her letter. She was glad he was finally coming home. She thought maybe if Marvin saw Cal around the house, he would think Cal was her man, and leave her alone.

Three nights after Cal got home, Granny got sick. She was sick for a few days, one night her fever spiked at one hundred and three degrees. Cal and Billy came to sit up with her all night. Edie had been sitting with her all day and refused to leave. Her fever dropped at daybreak, and Cal fell fast asleep on the floor next to her bed.

The next afternoon, Jock was waiting for Irene when she got to work. He began questioning her about Cal's whereabouts the night before. Irene told him about Granny and that she knew for a fact he had not left the house all night. Then she asked him why he wanted to know about Cal. "Marvin Maxwell was found hanging in his apartment this morning." Irene gasped. "The coroner said he had been dead since about four thirty this morning. He deemed it a suicide, but because he is one of Marcello's boys he wanted to check it out." "I hate for anyone to die like that, but I can't say I'm sorry he won't be bothering me anymore," she replied. "Yeah, it's tough all right, but I'm glad I can stop being your bodyguard!" he laughed as he left.

It was almost Christmas and Cal and Billy brought a huge Christmas tree for Jackie. Everyone had a hand in decorating it. Jackie didn't get her hopes up too much about Christmas. She was well aware that money was short and what money they did have would have to be spent on necessities. She knew if she didn't expect anything she wouldn't he disappointed. She was very proud of her tree and was happy to have what she had.

A few nights before Christmas, Curly was waiting for Irene after work. As she got to the first step, he stepped out of the shadows. Irene was so startled she screamed! When she realized it was him they both laughed. "What are you doing here?" she asked. "I wanted to see you and Jacqueline." he announced. "It's after two o'clock Curly, Jackie's been in the bed for hours! She goes to Sunday School in the morning and will have to get up early. I can't wake her now," she protested. "I know I just want to see her that's all," he said. "Well, come on in. want some coffee?" she offered. "Sure, sounds warm." He said rubbing his hands together and blowing the warmth of his breath on them." He told Irene he was in town on business as usual and just wanted to see them before he left. He sounded troubled, but Irene knew better than to ask questions, she just listened as he talked. He said he was sorry he hadn't been there when she needed him last year, and he knew she probably needed help financially right now to get back on her feet. She didn't say anything, just looked at him. He continued, "Has Jacqueline told you what she wants for Christmas?" "She doesn't say. She knows I can't afford much, so she doesn't ask. She's a good kid, Curly. She has a heart and wouldn't want me to feel bad because I couldn't buy her what she asked for. So she doesn't ask." He smiled and nodded, "Well, don't worry about it, she'll have what she wants. You know, Irene, I do love her and you. Someday I want to tell her. I want her to know that I had to protect her and you. I want to know her and her to know me. There will come a time I can tell her the truth about things, and I would appreciate it if you would let me be the one to explain my absence to her." "Sure, Curly whatever you say," she replied. He continued, "I have to leave Irene. I don't know how long I will be away." She stared at him as he continued, "I was hoping I would be able to spend some time with you before I left, but it isn't going to work out." She wanted to say that wasn't anything new, but she thought better of it considering his mood.

"You always pick the wrong guys, don't you, Babe?" he chuckled. She bowed her head knowing he was talking about Fred Anderson and Marvin Maxwell! "Well, that Maxwell person won't be bothering you or anybody else, he's been taken care of." Irene gasped, "What do you mean taken care of." "Let's just say he won't be 'hanging' around bothering you anymore." He answered half laughing. She said half laughing as well, "That wasn't funny, Curly." He spoke seriously, "Irene, you have to know that no matter what, I will make sure you and Jacqueline are always looked after. I will be watching, even if I'm not where you can see me. I always have been and I always will. Nothing happens that I don't know about. You know that." "Why are you talking like this? What's the matter?" she couldn't hold back any longer. She walked over to his chair and put her arms around his neck from behind, kissing the top of his head. He pulled her around in his lap and kissed her. They made mad passionate love followed by more of the same until both their bodies were in a state of total gratification and exhaustion.

The sun would be rising soon; he had to leave. "I'll see to Santa Claus for Jacqueline." He reminded her as he put on his pants. She lay breathless under the covers; tears streaming down her face. As he leaned to kiss her goodbye, he wiped her tears away, "I love you."

Before he left he quietly slipped into Jackie's room, bent down and kissed her on the cheek. Then he whispered, "Pop loves you, Baby. I'll see you tomorrow. Look for me at the filling station by a pretty blue car." She wriggled as if she were awakening. He left.

The next morning at breakfast, Jackie told Granny about the dream she had had. "It was so real, Granny, I could smell his perfume!" she said.

As she and Sally, the little girl from next door, were walking to Sunday school, Jackie told her about the dream. When they reached the corner Jackie said, "You look, Sally! I'm scared to! Sally grabbed her arm, "He's there, Jackie! Just like in your dream!" Jackie looked across the street, there leaning against a blue car was a man she just knew was her father. They stood starring at each other; finally he waved slightly. She threw up her hand and waved back, then she turned and ran home! When she got inside, she told Granny that the man in her dream was really there. "Sometimes our dreams are real and do have meanings, Jackie. Otherwise, how could any of them come true?" Granny said hugging her. Jackie knew her dream was real and she wished she had just walked up to him and made him tell her he was her father. She left the house running back to the filling station; he was gone. She kicked a pebble all the way home. She made up her mind the man was just a nice man waving at two little girls; it was just a dream.

The next day Uncle Cal and Billy brought Jackie a duck they had found on the beach. She played with the duck all day until her bedtime. She told them 'Herman' was the best Christmas present she had ever gotten! They helped her make a cage for Herman from some old window screens they found under the house. He seemed content in his new home.

The Saratoga closed early Christmas Eve, and about midnight Curly arrived with what looked like Santa's Toy Shop. He also had a turkey and all the trimmings for Christmas dinner. He stayed awhile taking some of the toys out of the boxes so she would see them first. When he had finished he said, "I'm leaving tonight, Irene. I've got to get going." "I know I shouldn't ask, but where are you going?" I'm not sure. I just know I'll be gone for awhile taking care of business. I wish I didn't have to go, I love you both, very much," he pulled her close to him and held her for the longest, and then he kissed her and walked to Jackie's room. He bent down, kissed her on the cheek, and said, "Daddy, loves you, Baby. Merry Christmas, angel." He stopped at the front door and kissed Irene, "Merry Christmas, sweetheart. "I really do love you both." With that he left. She went to the door to stop him, but locked it instead; she knew he couldn't stay.

Irene didn't sleep that night and was in the kitchen when the sun came up cooking their Christmas feast. When Jackie got up she followed the delicious smell into the kitchen. When she saw the turkey she began crying and saying, "Oh…Oh no! Oh no! Then she ran outside calling, Herman, Herman!" To her relief he was still quacking! She ran back as she stepped inside the living room she saw all the packages underneath the tree! A life–size doll, Easy Bake Oven, Candy Factory, a snow cone machine, and a brand new wardrobe! There was a card addressed to Irene, containing five crisp one hundred dollar bills. The note said, *Merry Christmas, Darling!*"

CHAPTER TEN

In the spring, Mikey offered Irene a house he owned on Marconi Street. He had been renting the house out and his tenants had moved. He made her an offer she couldn't refuse, no rent just maintain it and pay the utilities. If he ever decided to sell it, she would have first option.

It was a larger house than the old one, a two story wood frame house with hardwood floors, a fireplace in the living room, a huge kitchen and a screened in back porch. The best part was, it was still in the same neighborhood.

Cal, Billy, Gus, and Edie helped her pack, move, and then unpack at the new place. They had a paint party using paint Mikey had stored under the Saratoga.

Everything seemed to be going well for Irene, with the exception of missing Curly so much. Business had picked up at the bar, so her hours had increased. Cal and Gus seemed to be staying out of trouble, Granny was doing better, Jackie seemed happy. Only one thing could have made her life better, Curly.

Edie still helped Irene out with Jackie and Granny from time to time. She wasn't around too much after the move, as she had met a man from Georgia that was keeping her busy.

Irene had to keep Jackie occupied, especially since school was about to be out for the summer. She made a deal with Walter, the taxi driver that hung around the bar. He would take Jackie to events like the movie, skating, pick her up and see her safely home, and Irene would buy his drinks when he wasn't driving.

What's your pleasure?" she asked the customer without looking up. "How about a hello and a hug for an old friend?" the familiar voice requested. She looked up and smiled into the face of Joe Allums. She asked Mikey to take over for a few minutes while she took a break. She and Joe sat in the booth for awhile catching up on lost time and reminiscing about the past. "Have you seen Curly?" she asked. "Nah, I guess the last time I saw him was just before Christmas. You know his mother died and he was home for her funeral." "No, I didn't know that. I thought his father would go first," she said quietly. "Oh, he did. He drowned in the swimming pool last summer. I guess Guido is the last and then Curly will fill his shoes." "I didn't know about his father either. I never got to meet him or his uncle. Curly came to see me at Christmas; I could tell something was wrong, but you know him, he doesn't tell me things. I hope when something does happen to his uncle he will…well, you know. I guess I missed a lot while I was away." "Yeah, Curly told me what happened. I'm sorry, Irene. If I had known I would have helped you out." "Thanks, Joe, I know you would have. It was just one of those things where you do what you have to do. Can I buy you a drink?" "Sure, I've never been able to turn down a drink or a pretty girl," he said winking. She brought him a whiskey straight up, "I think I remembered correctly." "You did, thanks." "Well, how long are you in town?" "Don't know yet, gotta wait for a meeting." "Why don't you drop by before you leave? Jackie would love to see her Uncle Joe." "I'll try to do that," he said as he got up to leave. "Take care, Irene." "You too, Joe, and thanks for…everything." She didn't have to say what she was thanking him for; the expression on his face let her know he knew.

Joe's presence in town made the other families nervous. Jock kept coming in the bar asking Irene about him. "I don't know anything. Jock. He was here the other night to say hello and have a drink. I haven't seen or heard from him since then. What's the big deal? Why can't your boss just leave me alone!" she snapped. "I won't go to jail or be harassed this time, Jock. I'm tired of being hassled just because some mob boss wants to know what some other mob boss is doing. I'm sick of being arrested and aggravated just because someone wants me out of the way while they gun run, or worse in the establishment I happen to have to earn my money from!"

Irene you are overreacting again," Jock said. "Don't tell me that, Jock. The last time you said that I was arrested for prostitution, and I've never been like that with anybody but my husband! So don't tell me I'm overreacting!" He just laughed and left. The more she thought about it, the madder she became. The next day she went to the District Attorney to see if there was anything she could do to keep them from arresting and harassing her. He listened as she told him about the same thing she had said to Jock. The only difference was she named Trafficante, Marcello, and Patrillo. The DA leaned forward, smiling, "There is nothing you can do against the police or any other authority, you wouldn't stand a snowball's chance in hell of winning that kind of case. They're sovereign, in other words, they can't be sued." "Can't you write them a letter or something?" she asked angrily. "Not really. I think the best thing you can do is stay out of their way. I really don't see how you can do anything else." He stood up, shook her hand and ushered her out the door. She was exasperated! She knew by his sinister attitude he was in somebody's pocket and she had just named every family from Georgia to New Orleans!

The next night, Joe came in the bar with a wad of money for Irene, and a note that read, *'Make it livable. Love, C.'* She was glad Curly had sent her the money, but she was relieved he was all right. The house was looking good, but the upstairs was in bad need of a paint job! She had used the paint Mikey had given her for the downstairs.

Later that evening, 'suits' from some of the 'families' came in to the Saratoga for a poker game. Mikey told her to take their drink orders once an hour until closing. She did as he said and the tips were fantastic! When she took the last round in to them the game didn't appear to be going very well. She heard them talking as she set their drinks down. They were arguing over a 'shipment'. She tried to get out as quickly as possible, and just about the time she got to the door, one of the men pulled a gun and popped the other one. She turned around just in time to see the shooter put the gun back in his pocket. Getting a better look at the shooter she recognized him as one of the men that got off the yacht in New Orleans when she went to California. He was older, but it was him! When he realized she had seen what he did, he gave her the evil eye and motioned for Mikey to speak with her. "Irene, you shouldn't have turned around! Why did you turn around?" "The noise scared me, it was reflex Mikey, that's all, just reflex." "You had better take some time off and keep your mouth shut about this, remember the little monkey." "I won't say anything, Mikey. I promise." Still shaken from the shooting she found it hard to finish her work. She poured herself a shot of whiskey and downed it. The taste brought back bad memories, but the alcohol seemed to calm her nerves. She finished cleaning the bar, and got her things together to leave. The 'suits' had left from the back room and Mikey was trying to close up. "I won't be but a few minutes, I wish you would let me drive you home," he pleaded. "I don't mind waiting, I wasn't looking forward to going home alone anyway." He counted the register and turned out the lights, "You go ahead so I can lock up, I'll be right behind you." As she opened the door and stepped out, a car driving extremely fast came screeching down the street. Just as it got to the bar a hail of bullets blasted all around her! Mikey opened the door and pulled her to safety! "Oh my God! Oh my God!" she was screaming. Mikey was visibly shaken as well, "Irene! Are you all right? Here, let me see, they didn't get you anywhere did they?" Irene continued to scream, Mikey slapped her to shock her so she would stop screaming. "Irene, you have to calm down!" he said shaking her by the shoulders. "I…I will! Why did they do that, Mikey were they really after me?" "Irene what you saw here tonight was a murder. They have to have assurance that you will keep your mouth shut! No matter who questions you, you saw nothing and you heard nothing! Do you understand?" "Yes, Mikey, but that man…he works for Curl…" "Forget it, Irene! Damn it, there was no man! Nobody! You had better listen to me. Next time they won't be so generous! They missed on purpose!" he was shouting. "I understand, I swear I will not tell anyone, anything, no matter who asks." "Good girl. Now let's go," he commanded. When they walked out to the car it had been showered as well, "Damn it! I'll have a fucking hard time explaining this to my insurance company!" he said shaking his head. The body of the man shot in the poker game was sitting up in the passenger side of Mickey's car! That's my warning to keep quiet. You'd think after all these years they would know I'm not going to open my damn mouth! I know what they're capable of doing. I've seen it all and heard it all, and you better take this little warning seriously, Irene. We had better call a taxi. "Irene, I think it would be best for both of us if you took some time off. I think a couple or three weeks ought to be enough time for this to die down," he said as he pulled the roll of the night's take out of his pocket. He handed her three bills. "Thanks Mikey, I'm sorry about all this," she said. "Hell, Irene it's not really your fault. You didn't do anything, but your job. I'm just sorry I can't work you for a few weeks. Now I'll have to work!" He winked at her hoping to get a smile. He succeeded.

Irene used her time off to paint the bedrooms. She and Jackie moved a mattress into the living room floor, Granny's room was already downstairs, and so she didn't have to worry about the fumes bothering her. "We can pretend we're camping out," she told Jackie. Jackie loved the games her mother made up, and was thrilled with this one!

A car horn tooted in the front yard, Jackie ran to the door and started to open it. "NO!" Irene yelled, "Don't open that door until we know who it is!" Jackie was upset because Irene had yelled at her. "Come here, Baby. I'm sorry I yelled at you, but we have to be careful about opening doors since we are three ladies here alone." Jackie smiled because her mother had called her a lady. The horn blew again. Irene went out the back and peeked around the corner to see who was there. She recognized Joe as he got out of his car. She breathed a sigh of relief and went back into the house and opened the door, as he was coming up the stairs. "I don't give curb service, Joe. Sorry," she teased. "Ha! Ha!" he said as he sat down on the top step, "Where's my girl?" "She's in the house, but I don't know if she will remember you." She called for Jackie. "Hey, cutie, remember me? Uncle Joe." "I remember you. You have my name stamped on your arm. "Did it wash off?" she asked. "Come look and see," he said. She went over to him and he raised his sleeve so she could see. "Nope, it didn't wash off." "Does it hurt?" "Not now. It did when I first got it, though," he admitted. "Mama does yours hurt?" "No!" Irene answered emphatically. "I didn't know you had a tattoo, Irene. Where is it?" he asked snickering. "Somewhere you'll never see. Can we change the subject, please." They all laughed. "Miss Jacqueline would you do your old Uncle Joe a favor? She nodded. "I think I dropped my keys, will you get me a flashlight?" "Sure," she answered. Irene began looking on the ground between the car and the stairs where the porch light shone. They were not there. "Mama and me are good at hide and seek, we'll find the keys for you. Won't we Mama?" "Yeah, sure we will. Bring me the light." Irene opened the drivers door, Jackie leaned in first and Irene over her. No keys. Irene pulled the front seat forward and when she did she saw the bloody body of a badly beaten dark haired woman, lying across the seat. She gasped and pushed Jackie out of the car. "Mama who is that sleeping in the backseat? "Nobody you know, just a friend of Uncle Joe. You go on in the house, now." "Ok. Goodnight, Uncle Joe." "Goodnight, sweet pea," he said hugging her. She hated having to go to bed now. She wished Granny and Mama would stop sending her out of the room when things were getting interesting. She could tell by the look on her mama's face that she was angry, and she sure wished she could watch!

"How dare you bring this to my home, Joe! What on earth were you thinking? Jackie shouldn't be exposed to that stuff and I don't appreciate you bringing it here! In fact, Joe, I'm shocked you would! I thought more of you than that and I thought you felt the same." She was nearly screaming. "I'm sorry Irene. I just do as I'm told." "What do you mean by that?" "I've gotta go Irene. You just be careful, ok. I'll be seeing you." She stomped up the stairs and slammed the door before he was in the car. Then she leaned against the door crying. "Mama why are you crying? Did you and Uncle Joe have a fight because the lady was sleeping in his car?" Jackie asked. "No, I'm just tired that's all. Let's fix the bed and go to sleep." While they were making the bed, the phone rang, "Irene, you've been warned! Keep your mouth shut about what you saw in the bar and stay out of the District Attorney's office. Bad things happen to women that talk too much!" he hung up. She began crying again because she recognized the voice on the other end...it was Curly!

A few days later, the newspaper ran a picture of a dead woman that had washed up on the rocks underneath the Twenty Second Street Causeway. The headline read, "Do you know Jane Doe?" When Irene and Granny saw the picture they recognized her, it was Edie! Irene called the authorities to identify her, but they said they knew who she was and that a man was in custody for her murder. Irene tried to tell them they were wrong...the phone went dead. She knew she was being listened to, and she was afraid. A short time later the phone rang, "Irene, I told you not to get involved! Now other bad things will happen. I'm afraid for you and Jacqueline!" he sounded upset, "Don't underestimate these people, Irene. You know they have ways of getting rid of situations and people they feel are in the way. You'd better listen to me, you know I wouldn't lie to you." He hung up. Irene lit a cigarette and went out on the porch. She didn't want her mother or Jackie to see her this upset.

A neighborhood kid everyone called 'Cracker Boy' came by to see Irene. He was a seventeen– year old James Dean wannabe. He was blonde, blue eyed, with muscles and dimples. He was the boy next door you wouldn't want to take home to mama! All the girls from nine to nineteen had a crush on him, including Jackie! Cracker Boy was taken, however by a ponytailed cutie named Susie. He and Susie would take the neighborhood kids to the park, skating, or to the movies. Irene trusted him. She saw through his tough guy exterior. He was on his own for the most part. His father had never been around, and his mother was drunk most of the time. Sometimes when she was drunk she became abusive and Cracker Boy couldn't go home. Irene would let him sleep on the screened–in porch if it were warm enough and on the livingroom couch if not. Irene was like his second mother so to speak. Today, she was the one in need; she decided to confide in him. I'm being watched by the FBI." He laughed believing she was being facetious. "Here, I'll prove it." She flipped him a dime, "Go across the street and call me. When I answer, say, Irene, are you packed and ready to leave?" "I'll answer 'yes' and then you hang up and run back here as fast as you can." He did as she asked and before he could get back to the house an unmarked car pulled up and two men got out. "You're not planning to go anywhere, now are you, Irene?" one of them asked. "No, I just wanted to see how long it would take you boys to get here." They left laughing. Irene wasn't, she was scared.

When they left, Irene told Cracker Boy she needed to get away for awhile. He told her not to worry he would take care of everything.

The next day Cracker Boy and Susie took Jackie to the movies. Irene went to Cal and Billy's for awhile. When she saw the unmarked car go down the street the second time she knew they were not parking and watching her. After explaining to Cal where she was going, and making sure he would go or send Gus to stay with Granny, she slipped out the back door and down the street to where Cracker Boy's car was parked. She crawled in the backseat and laid down. A few minutes later Cracker Boy, Susie, and Jackie joined her. They headed for Jacksonville.

Irene had enough money to rent a motel room for a month and very little for food and whatever else they might need. Three weeks had passed and all they had been able to afford was bologna and bread. Irene was depressed because she didn't know exactly what she would do next. She was outside watching Jackie play with some children who were also staying at the motel. The smell of fried fish filled the air. It made Irene hungry, and she knew Jackie must have been feeling the same. She swallowed her pride and followed the smell, knocked on the door praying the occupant would be friendly. A lady came to the door and smiled as Irene said pointing, "Excuse me, my daughter and I are staying across the way. I believe she is playing with your children on the swings." "Oh, yes, you're Jackie's mother," she replied. "Yes, that's right. The reason I came by was to ask if you have extra fish would you allow Jackie to have it. I wouldn't ask for myself, but we have been eating bologna and bread for three weeks." Irene bowed her head in embarrassment. Smiling the lady asked, "Want you come in for something cold to drink?" Irene accepted. When she had finished her tea she excused herself to check on the children. She thanked the lady and left. She called Jackie to go inside, it was time to bathe and settle down for the evening. While Jackie was in the tub a knock came at the door, there stood the lady with two paper plates of food, a box of cereal, milk, peanut butter and jelly, and a fresh loaf of bread. "Thank you so much! I wish I could pay you. If there is anything I can do for you while you are here, please let me know." "There is nothing. Enjoy the fish. Goodnight." "Goodnight, and thanks again." The lady waved as she went down the stairs. Irene closed the door and cried. Jackie came out of the bathroom, "Mama, why are you crying?" "Pride goes before a fall, Jackie. You always remember that," she said with a smile. Jackie looked bewildered, shrugged her shoulders and began eating.

The next day, another knock came at the door. This time it was Gus. Irene was shocked to see him and was afraid he had bad news. Her first thought was of her mother, she was wrong. He was bearing bad news, however, their sister, Marie had been murdered in Georgia. She had been beaten with a baseball bat, stuffed in an old trunk, and left to die in an abandoned apartment. She had been dead nearly a week.

Gus drove them back to Tampa. Granny was very upset about Marie, but was not well enough to go to the funeral. Billy and Jackie stayed with Granny while Cal, Gus, and Irene went to Georgia.

When they returned, Irene received another phone call, "Irene, you can run, but you can't hide forever. When they want to find you they will. I told you something bad would happen if you talked. I'm sorry about Marie. Please listen to me this time!" she slammed the phone down as hard as she could. She couldn't tell her mother or brothers that Marie was murdered because of her, she just couldn't!

Irene went back to work at the Saratoga. She worked hard, but didn't hang around too much after hours. She was still scared. Mikey would let her off when he knew the 'suits' were coming in so they wouldn't see her there. He knew they were aware she was working, they knew everything, but he didn't want to flaunt the fact.

Gus, Cal, or Billy would come for her nearly every night that they were not off working or doing God knows what. She felt better having someone see her home.

Irene had noticed the authorities weren't harassing her. She was glad they were not questioning her about the shooting. Mikey had told her they probably didn't know about it, and wouldn't care anyway because he was mob connected, "The mob has their own justice system. They take care of their own, good or bad."

Granny's health began to worsen. Billy was good about taking care of her when Irene had to work. When she wasn't working, Irene took care of her. She would have done anything to keep Granny at home. The thoughts of her being in a nursing home were unacceptable to Irene.

One night after everyone was asleep, Granny got out of bed unassisted and fell. Her yelling for help awakened Irene. She was taken by ambulance to Tampa General Hospital where a few days later she succumbed to a blood clot in her lung.

Irene had never known pain like she felt with the loss of her mother, the only person she could always count on to be there. She felt so alone. Jackie was hurting too, but together she and Irene would go on.

Irene wished she could see Curly. She needed him to comfort her and tell her that everything would be all right. She would have comforted him had she known about the death of his father and mother, if only he had come to her.

A few days after Granny's funeral a dozen red roses arrived for Irene. The card read, "*I'm sorry about your mother. She was a great lady and I respected and loved her very much. Love, C.*"

CHAPTER ELEVEN

In 1967, reports began to surface that the FBI was not continuing to actively investigate Kennedy's assassination. Hoover had made open promises to continue to investigate as long as there was doubt as to who really killed JFK.

Also, about this time, Mob boss Carlos Marcello, began bragging about having had Kennedy killed. There were no reports of any of this in the FBI files. The only tie anyone could make with Marcello and Oswald, Kennedy's supposed assassin was the fact that Oswald had lived in New Orleans.

Several stories were floating the bar regarding the man that murdered Oswald, Jack Ruby. He owned a nightclub in Dallas and was supposedly on the payroll of one of the 'families'; in these tales, the name of the family was conveniently whispered, left out, or referred to as 'mob connected'.

Hoover was getting restless with the Warren Commission and their investigation into Kennedy's death. He initiated his own investigation into every member of the Warren Commission for his 'private and confidential' files, as insurance. His restlessness was like a wave of nausea to the 'outsiders' under his thumb, and like the domino effect, the higher echelon began to pay visits to their constituents to make sure they kept their mouths shut about any business to which they might be privy. In Tampa and New Orleans several prostitutes washed ashore as warnings, bar room brawls and confrontations ended in killings. The shrimp boats were not making gun runs, but some of the crew members were meeting with 'accidents'.

The attorney that had been assigned to represent Irene at her trial met with an untimely death, when his car was blown up as he turned the ignition. His office was burned in the aftermath.

Jock had warned Irene, "I've got a feeling shit is fixing to hit the fan! You need to take some time off." She reminded him she had a child to support and her job was what kept food on their table. She knew something bad would probably happen, Jock's feelings had never been wrong before, and she knew with all that was happening he was not wrong now.

A few days after her conversation with Jock, she received a note, *'Backstairs, 2:00a.m. ,C.'* she wasn't sure meeting him was such a good idea. She laughed to herself as she thought,' What else is new?' She knew he was like a drug to her, an addiction; she knew she would be there.

As she exited the bar she could see him standing on the stairs smoking a cigarette. He looked the same as the first time she ever remembered seeing him! She dreaded him seeing her, she felt as if she had aged twenty years since her mother's death. However, the first words out if his mouth were, "You're looking good, Irene." His words caused her to blush, as she had when she was thirteen. He stepped aside and motioned her up the stairs into the apartment. She had made up her mind she was not going to allow him to touch her. She wanted this meeting to stay 'friendly'.

When they were inside he sat on the sofa and patted the seat beside him for her to join him. She sat on the other end instead. He chuckled at her obviousness. "How have you and Jacqueline been since your mother's death? he asked concerned. "It's been hard for both of us. There are times I still think about telling her something, or I'll wake up and start to go check on her. It's horrible, Curly! Jackie misses her so much. If it were not for Billy, I don't know what we would do. He watches her while I work." "Yeah, I know, I hate it for both of you," he said. "How are you? Joe told me about your folks, I'm sorry. Why didn't you let me know, Curly. I would have been here for you." "I wasn't as close to my folks as you were to yours. I miss knowing they're around, but I wasn't really close to either of them. You know I was gone from home a long time. I mostly saw them on Christmas and when I was summoned. Uncle Guido is on his deathbed, that's why I'm here." "Oh, I...I didn't know," she said not wanting to lie and say she was sorry. The only thing she was sorry about was that he lived as long as he did! She knew he was the main reason they were never allowed to live together as a real 'family'! "I will be leaving soon, Irene. When I leave this time, I won't be back," he said seriously. "Why?" she stammered. "What I have to tell you is confidential. You must promise me you will never discuss it with anyone and that you'll never turn on me, Irene. You've already seen what happens when people talk, it's not pretty." She nodded. "When Guido dies I am turning over information about my family and the other families to Edgar. He has promised to see that I am sent someplace safe under an assumed name. I wish I could take you and Jacqueline with me, but it's too dangerous for all of us. When you hear of my death, act sorrowful. You will know it's not true. Hell, the public already thinks I'm dead, thanks to Hollywood, so it is only in 'family' circles that it will matter or come up anyway. A lot of people will go down, Irene. Maybe not right away, but eventually because of what I'm doing, truths about a great many things will be made public." "But, why do you have to leave? Why can't you just stay here and live?" she said as she inched closer to him. "I'll be the head of the Patrillo Family when Guido dies. That makes me an automatic target! The other families will see to it I don't live to conduct business as the head of the family. They're too stupid to realize I mean them no harm and could care less about 'family' business." he explained. "Why can't you call a meeting and tell them that?" she asked childlike. He chuckled, "It doesn't work like that. I know too much on all of them. They're too afraid and loyalty is what it's all about, Irene. It just wouldn't work; they'd shoot me as I left the meeting, hell they would probably shoot me before I left. It's better this way, for everybody. The best thing you could do is get out of Tampa! You have been harassed all these years because of me and when I leave it will get worse because of our relationship. Jackie will not be safe, hell, Cal will even be in danger." She was devastated by his words. She tried to listen carefully to what he was saying, but suddenly her heart had stopped and when it dawned on her he really wasn't coming back her heart began racing to catch up! He had been away for long periods before, but she always knew he would be back. Now he was telling her this! "Irene, I'm sorry, but you and Jackie have to leave. Go somewhere and change your names!"

Her mind was not absorbing what he was saying, her ears were ringing and his words sounded like echoes. Finally she put her hands over her ears and began shaking her head, "STOP! STOP! Don't say anymore. I can't hear anymore! Why can't we just be normal, why can't you just..." Before she could finish he moved closer putting his arms around her, "Listen, Irene, this is serious fucking business! It's not about us! It's about you and Jacqueline. It's about fucking safety and that's all!" "Ok, we'll move! I'll just uproot our child from everything and everybody she knows and we'll move! That's just one more way your family has screwed us Curly! One more way to make Jackie suffer for our mistakes! Where should we move Curly? she shouted. "I don't know. I can't tell you where to go. Hell, I don't even know where I'll be! Edgar has your number, too. He wants the tape that was made at the studio party. You remember that party, don't you, Irene?" He asked in an almost threatening tone. She nodded. "There were some very influential people there doing some very bad things. He wants the tape before anyone else gets it, and for insurance. That tape will not be destroyed because the party was filmed on the end of an old movie that the critics are calling a classic. Edgar promised to keep it safe and under wraps until this Kennedy shit blows over. Then he said it wouldn't matter who was fucking who at the party." He kind of laughed, "Hell, Edgar probably wants to watch it with his queer ass partner for an aphrodisiac! He would probably get off on it! I have to give him what he wants, Irene. It's the only way he will assure me he will leave you alone and help Jackie when the time comes." Looking confused she continued to listen. "Someday when she is older, I will send for her. If she wants to come, don't try to stop her. If I live through all of this, I want to explain everything to her myself. I've talked to some people that will help Jacqueline, go to school or whatever she wants. It might be best if you don't say anything to her, let her make up her own mind. I've had to live my whole life with someone telling me every move to make. It's wrong, Irene. Let her be independent, promise me that much, he said as he laid his head on her chest like a little child. She stroked his face as she said, "I promise, darling." He stroked her breasts, "Sweet and Sour, what a perfect description of our relationship, huh, Babe? I guess it's been more sour than sweet. I regret the hell out of that! I never wanted anything as much as I wanted us. I will never get over what my family did to us, that's why I am doing this. I refuse to pay for what else they have done and when Guido dies it will fall to me to clean up his mess. I want no part of it!" he held her as close as he could. "What about Joe, Curly? What will happen to Joe?" "Joe's a big boy now, he'll take care of himself. I doubt he'll hang around here; it will be too dangerous. Maybe he'll go somewhere, change his name, get a decent job and settle down. Who knows?" "I hope he will be all right." He grabbed her, pulled her as close to him as possible, "Don't forget who loves you, Irene. You're mine no matter where I am or where you are. I want to tell our daughter that I was there more than just that one time she saw me. I've known every scraped knee and burn, every big or little accomplishment she has ever had. I will still know. I will still have eyes as close to you as your skin! You'll never be without my eyes on you, I promise." Tears began streaming down his face onto her neck. She didn't know what to say; her heart was breaking. She began to cry, too. He got up taking her hand and together they lay on the bed where they continued to cry until they fell asleep.

The morning light caught them. Because of the danger they faced being seen together, they remained in the apartment all day. Irene awoke to his starring at her. He kissed her, and her plans for not allowing him to touch her were cast to the wind.

Their attraction had not subsided, if anything it had intensified! Before they realized what was happening, they were unbuttoning each other's clothes. She felt something under his shirt that alarmed her; it was a holstered gun! Their passion was interrupted, "What are you doing with that thing!" she protested. "Don't get all fired up, Irene it's just for protection. I've always had one, you just didn't know it, he said as he got up to hang it over the chair. Then he kissed her again. The touch of her body made him hornier than he could remember. He touched her neck and slowly descended to her breasts. Her nipples were hard and inviting, he kissed them, his touch made her back arch as she allowed his hardness to penetrate her. She kissed his shoulder, his chest, his lips; she wanted him to melt inside her as she pulled him closer, until she could hardly breathe. "More, More!" she begged breathlessly, as he pounded her body with his. She wrapped her legs around him as he exploded inside her. Neither had ever felt so much pleasure, while their hearts felt so much pain. Both knew this would be the last time they would make love. It would be remembered.

Their bodies were in a state of total gratification, satisfaction, and exhaustion. When he regained his strength he got up to take a shower. She lay sleeping. When she awoke he was gone. "Goodbye, I love you forever, C." was scrawled across the mirror with her lipstick. Five hundred dollars lay on the night table. She showered, cried, screamed, dressed…and went home.

Irene was confused and afraid. She knew Curly wouldn't lie about Jackie and her being in danger. Most of her life had been spent in Tampa. She worried about Cal, but couldn't warn him, she felt as though she were his Judas! She had no one to turn to, but Mikey or Jock. She wondered just how much she could trust either of them. She decided to talk to Mikey about leaving. She had no idea where to go, how she would get there, or what kind of work she would find. He told her when she decided what to do and would not be making her next shift to serve him a margarita, (a drink he would not usually order). He would then slip her pay into her purse.

That night the J.E. Straits Carnival opened, and after hours Mikey asked her to stay and serve the carnies. She was glad to make the extra money. Cal and Billy were there and got into a card game in the back with them. Cal won three games, enough to wipe out the other's money. On the fourth game the owner of the shows 'snake pit', put it in the pot. Cal won that, too!

When he took Irene home, he told her about winning, "A damn snake pit!" She asked him what he planned to do with it. "Hell, I have no idea. There's so much damn crap going on around here these days, I've about decided it might do me good to get the hell out of here awhile. Me and Billy need a change of scenery. I kind of like the idea of not staying in one place too long, if you know what I mean." She did know what he meant. "How about Jackie and me coming with you?" I need to work until Mikey finds someone else, but I like the idea of getting away, too. Things haven't been the same around here since Mama died. Do you think Gus would consider going?" "Yeah, he'll do whatever I do, you know that," he laughed.

The next day Cal lumbered into the bar with a black eye and burst lip. He flopped down on the first barstool he came to. Irene winced when she looked at his swollen face, "What happened to you?" "Well, what does it look like? I been in a damn fight!" "Where? With who?" "Down at that pool joint where all the niggers and white trash hang out. You know the place."

"Yeah, sometimes Cracker Boy and Susie take Jackie there to shoot pool. The place seems all right, Cal. He doesn't allow drinking, it's just somewhere for the kids to go to stay out of trouble," she said. "Well, I don't think he'll be in the neighborhood much longer," he snickered. "Why, what have you done, Cal?" she asked again. "Who the hell said I 'Did' anything? I just happen to know the sheets went in last night and put him out of business. He ought to know better than to cater to them fuckin' niggers anyway. If I'd known you'd been lettin' Jackie hang out in that place I'd put a stop to it before now," he retorted. "Cal, you're so bad! Why do you have to involve yourself with groups of people that just keep you in trouble? What are your plans if you leave town?" "Billy and I are gonna hook up with that carnival and run that snake show," he said proudly. "What do you know about running something like that? Aren't those snakes dangerous?" she asked. "Hell, if you're not scared of 'em, they won't hurt you. I thought about asking you to let Jackie go and work in it sometime." "I don't know, Cal. Jackie might be too afraid of it. I'll have to talk to her and think about it." "Well, you better do some fast talking and thinking, we leave here in two days. Here's another thought for you, who's gonna look after Jackie this summer with Billy gone?" "I said I would think about it, Cal!" she snapped. "Ah, come on, sis. You can't look after her and work, and Cracker Boy don't need to be playin' 'mommy' to her! You see he takes her to places like that pool hall, where they let niggers and everything else in!" he begged. "Everything else, like the KKK! You have no right to talk about people, Cal!" she was aggravated with his attitude. "Don't push it, Calvin! I'll think about it! No promises!" she walked off to get something out of the storeroom, as she was walking she commanded, "Go home, Cal! Jackie's at your place with Billy; I have to work until three. I'll get her sometime in the morning." She stuck her head out of the storeroom door, "And Cal, don't even mention this to Jackie or the answer is no! I'll talk to her myself." When she returned, he was gone.

Jock came in around midnight when he was off duty. He told Irene that Trafficante's boys were in town. He didn't tell her anything else, but somehow she knew it was a warning.

She thought about what Curly and Cal had said, and what Jock was saying. She didn't fear for herself, just Jackie.

The next day she talked to Gus about helping her pack and get ready to leave, and then they would join Cal, Billy and Jackie at the end of the month. He agreed. Then she talked to Jackie about going to work for Cal in the carnival, and that she and Gus would join them in about a month. Jackie was so excited. She had no idea what she was about to face.

Making Cal give her a schedule of their stops and promising to let Jackie call whenever she wanted, she agreed to let her go. Irene was sad when they left, but she knew Jackie would be safer this way and she would join them soon.

A week after they left, Cal called, "Irene, Jackie can't handle these damn snakes! Hell, she won't even get in the fucking pit; she walks around the edge of the damn thing! Will you talk to her?" He handed the phone to Jackie. "Hey, Mama," she said sniveling. "Baby, what's the matter? Are you all right?" Irene asked. "Uncle Cal put me in that pit and then he threw a handful of those snakes on me! I didn't like it Mama, I was scared. I want to come home!" Cal yelled out loud enough for Irene to hear, "You ain't nothing but a big ole baby! Them Damn snakes ain't gonna bother you! You know I'd kill any son of bitch that hurt you whether it was a real snake or the two legged kind! She's just being silly, Irene! Tell her she's just being silly." "Tell him to shut up." "Sticking her tongue out at Cal Jackie said, "Mama said for you to shut up Uncle Cal!" "Tell Cal I will come work the pit. I will try to leave this weekend. Don't get back in that pit until I get there, Jackie. Everything will be all right, Baby. I promise."

The next night she served Mikey a margarita. When she left she hugged him and slipped a note of thanks into his pocket. He had slipped her pay into her purse along with an extra one hundred dollar bill and a note that said, *"I'll miss you, Irene. You know where to find me if you ever need me. I was told if you wanted to leave town to give you this bill. You know where I got it. Take care of yourself and Jackie. Love, Mikey."*

She cried as she packed her bags. The next day she caught a bus to Orlando. Gus stayed to finish storing their things until they knew how the carnival would treat them.

The bus ride was a good chance for Irene to think. She thought about all the times she had been with Curly, their marriage, their lovemaking, her tattoos she now wore like war wounds, and all the things he had said to her and promised her. Her heart was telling her she would never see him again, and this time her head was listening. She had no regrets because she loved him then and she knew in her heart she always would. However, she knew she had to let go. She was all cried out, the denial was over, the grieving was subsiding, now she had to live with the fact that he was gone, dead to her, and move on. She knew he was not over for Jackie, but she couldn't dwell on that. She had to bury her past before it consumed her. She would be safe in the carnival because she would be moving around and nobody would know her. She was looking forward to not having to look over her shoulder every minute. She would survive and she would go on, without him. Although she was getting on with her life, there was a certain part of her that had died when Curly left. She had a numbness that allowed her to accept things she would have never considered in the past. She didn't want Jackie to want for anything, or miss out on life in any way. She would keep her promise to Curly and let Jackie make her own decisions about her life, so she would not have regrets when she was older. She also knew if Curly were alive he would keep his promise to tell Jackie about things he wanted her to know.

CHAPTER TWELVE

Irene worked hard managing the snake pit. She had a real knack for handling reptiles. It seemed her picture was featured in the newspapers in nearly every town they stopped. She didn't want to be recognized so she bought a long wig, a jungle Jane leopard print outfit, a straw hat with a big flower, and drew her lipstick around the outside of her lips. In some cities Cal had authorities breathing down his back because they believed Irene to be retarded. In one city the authorities came to shut the show down and take Irene away! Irene watched the argument as if she were watching a tennis match. Finally she cleared her throat, they took notice as she wiped the lipstick off, pulled off the wig and hat, and said, "How dare you have the audacity to question my veracity!" Realizing she was as sane as they, the show was allowed to continue.

Jackie went to work as a mime robot that was the draw to the Wax Museum. She was making good money for a thirteen year old, and she liked it better than working with the reptiles. Like her mother, her body disguised her youth. Along with a bust she had developed an attitude and a taste for cigarettes.

Besides the Wax Museum, she worked the 'joints', which were the games on the midway, the basketball throw, and the balloon and dart games. One day while working the dart game, a young black woman reached over the counter and tried to pull the money apron off Jackie. Jackie took a dart and stuck the woman's hand to the counter! Because of continued racial rioting, the carnival owners decided it would behoove them to put Jackie up in a motel for the remainder of the gig. Jackie enjoyed being treated like a princess with a poolside room, room service, and color television. The boxcar they slept in did not afford them such niceties. When the carnival moved on, Jackie was given the job of selling tickets. She didn't like that job as much as the joints, and the money wasn't as good.

Irene had shown Jackie how to handle the snakes, telling her that they sensed she was afraid of them and that could cause them to be aggressive. She didn't make her handle them, instead she waited until Jackie was ready and just picked one up on her own. Jackie became accustomed to them and realized she had power over them. Her fear grew into respect for the reptiles just as Irene had said.

Cal had made a name for himself around the carnival as a 'bad ass'. He was feared for his temper and his reputation and threats preceded him when new carnies came around, which was quite often in the carnival business. Cal had seen to it Jackie was off limits to the carnies. He got them all together and warned them, "The first one of you sons of bitches that touch my niece will be pushing up daisies from the bottom of the deep blue sea!" They believed him and steered clear.

Once, in the middle of the night Billy had heard something in the pit and came out with a cocked gun ready to shoot! he was mortified when he saw it was Jackie! She had to explain her sleeping in the pit, since she couldn't say she was afraid Gus would sneak in her boxcar to molest her, she said she was afraid someone would break in the trailer on her.

After that Cal decided the carnival train might be too accessible and bought Irene a two–bed camper and Jackie didn't have to worry about Gus or anyone else breaking in her boxcar.

Carnival life was proving to be good for all of them. A year passed with no word from Curly. That part of Irene's life was over and working long hours outdoors in the heat left very little time to think about the past. She did occasionally dream about the good times, the bad were melting away. She was as happy as she would ever be again.

Selling tickets or working in a grab joint (food trailer), was getting boring for Jackie. She was offered a job with friends of Gus, Clara and Harry

Snow. They owned a girly show, the Top Hat, which ran with the carnival. If a spot would not allow a strip show, they would perform at the nearest military base. The strippers were allowed to wear pasties and g–strings.

Jackie was a very pretty girl with long strawberry blonde hair, azure eyes, and a few freckles scattered across her nose. In the show she wore a blonde or platinum wig, an emerald green sequined dress with long gloves, and high heels. The pasties were homemade to match her dress. She wore a panel of fringe over the g–string which could allow the customers a peek at their pubic hairs if the girls wanted to make extra money.

Harry, the barker for the show would also fix the girls a couple of strong drinks to relax them so they would dance less inhibited. He and Clara were good to their girls, putting them up in the best hotels, paying all their expenses, plus a salary.

Jackie had just been with the show for a short time when they went to Virginia. After the show in Arlington, Jackie and Danny, a roadie for the show, were looking for a place to eat. A soldier walked up and started a conversation with them. They explained they were looking for a place to get a bite to eat. He told them there was a fast food burger joint across the golf course, "Come on. I'll show you," he said. They walked around the corner of the building and he pointed in the opposite direction Danny was looking. When Danny turned to look, he kicked him across the lower back and Danny fell to the ground. As Jackie was bent down to help him, the soldier grabbed her from behind, placing one arm around her neck; with the other hand he held a knife to her throat. He told Danny, "Stay put. I won't hesitate to cut her throat!" He dragged Jackie by her waist length hair around the back of the building into what looked to her as the wicked forest. He slapped her down onto the hard frozen ground and straddled her, using his knife to cut the straps of her clothes. He pulled her panties off and threw them aside. He pressed the cold blade of the knife against her throat as he commanded her to unzip his pants and pull them down. Then barley scratching her throat with the knife blade he ordered her to take his penis out of his underwear. Just as he was about to penetrate her, she saw lights in the distance, "Look! The police!" she shouted. He jumped up with his pants around his ankles, pulling them up as he ran into the night. She did not stop to find her clothes, she ran in the cold darkness toward the lights. It was the NCO Club.

A friendly black woman, who had been performing, was standing outside the door when she ran up. Immediately, the woman slipped off the black pants she was wearing beneath a long tunic, and gave them to her, the doorman took off his coat and wrapped it around her.

While all of this was going on Danny had gotten back to the carnival, he and some of the carnies had the soldier and had beaten him to a pulp. The Military Police Officer offered one of them his Billy Club, but he declined saying they didn't want to kill him just make him remember what he had done to Jackie for the rest of his life. Jackie was taken to the infirmary where she was treated for abrasions and asked questions about the incident. When they were finished, one of the carnies went in to see her. He informed her the soldier was in custody and would be in a line–up. He explained it was to her advantage not to identify him to the authorities. He also said, "Don't try to recognize him, he is very badly beaten and you'll have nightmares!" She wanted him to pay the maximum for what he had done so she identified him.

The Military Police talked her out of pressing charges against the man because of her age and the fact that she was a stripper. He said they knew who he was and assured her he would be punished, military style.

Although Gus had molested Jackie from the time she could remember, this was different. The soldier did not follow through with his dastardly deed, but the violence with which he mauled her was gruesome and the evil in his eyes would haunt her forever.

After the attack she became withdrawn believing she had in some ways caused it. She refused to go to work for Top Hat. Irene worried about her, but didn't know how to help her. She stayed with Irene for a few weeks trying to get over the nightmares and the bad feelings.

Jackie made peace with herself about Gus, and she had decided he was never going to manipulate her again. She thought if she could face that demon she would be all right. Not being able to explain her reasoning for leaving, she decided to be gone before her mother got off work.

She took the money she made at the Top Hat, wrote a note for her mother, and left. She knew the name of the smaller show Gus had joined and the last stop they had made. She would hitch hike there and look for fliers telling the carnival's next stop. It took her two days to locate the carnival, and two more to get to it. When she arrived, Gus was surprised to see her. He made her call the carnival headquarters and leave a message for Irene to let her know she was all right. It might take a week for her to get the message, but he knew she would want to know.

She spent the night in Gus's trailer. She had found a pipe around the carnival and when she went to bed she put it through the door handle where Gus couldn't open it. When he came to the trailer for the night and couldn't get in, she yelled out the window, "Forget it Uncle Gus! I'm off limits forever! I wish I would get kidnapped and taken far away, so you're no threat to me anymore. I am also not passed killing somebody myself! So, if I were you…I'd leave me the hell alone!" He replied, "Well, where am I supposed to sleep?" "Try the snake pit! I've had to sleep in one before and it's not half bad! See you in the morning!" Gus slept under the trailer until daylight, then, he got out from underneath the trailer and went hunting some coffee. "I've got to find her a damn job! I'm too old for this sleeping under the damn stars shit!" he said aloud as he walked along rubbing his backside!

Jackie slept better that night than she had ever remembered. She had faced her demon and knew he would never bother her again! When she got up she went for breakfast, too. A young man who was a male stripper was sitting at the bar next to her and began talking. He told her all about the show he worked for. She told him about having worked for the Top Hat. He told her he could probably get her on with his show.

Lonnie and Monique Barrett ran a show similar to the Top Hat. They did not allow their girls to wear pasties or g–strings, but they paid for all meals, hotel rooms, bought all the clothes, Merle Norman make–up, and paid her two hundred dollars a week. They treated their employees like family and made sure they were never anywhere the customers could bother them. Like the Top Hat, they played the carnival when they could and military bases when they couldn't.

When the Straits Carnival went to Winter Haven for the off–season, Irene decided to go back to Tampa for a visit. She had been away for quite awhile, and wanted to see Mikey and Jock.

Mikey was alone when she walked into the Saratoga. He was so glad to see her. She had to tell him all about Jackie, but he still did not want her to tell him where she had gone or what she was doing. He was glad she was safe and things were working out for her. He asked her if she ever heard from Curly. "No, not since the last time he was here," she said softly and sadly. He told her from grapevine talk, Curly had just disappeared. Nobody was talking much anymore, he said. She asked about Jock. "Yeah, he's still around. Still chasing the crooks!" he laughed. Irene asked if Jock came in much, and he told her usually about midnight he made a round through the bar. She said she believed she would wait to see him. The bar had changed some, Mikey was now serving food, in addition to mixed drinks. He said chuckling, "You know how it is, Irene. You gotta keep up with the times or you get left behind." She placed her order and she and Mikey sat talking between his managerial duties, waiting for Jock. She wasn't disappointed, about a quarter til twelve he ambled in; not seeing her at first, Mikey pointed to the booth where she was sitting. He smiled as he walked over to her, "It's good to see you, Irene. How are you?" "Been good, Jock, you?" "Oh, you know how it is around here, always something going on, never a dull moment!" he replied. They talked about recent happenings and people they knew. He bought her a drink and they continued to talk. "Do you see much of Joe Allums?" she asked. "You didn't hear?" she shook her head no. Her heart jumped into her throat as he said, "Joe's car went off into the Bay a year or so ago. His body was never recovered, but the coroner said he probably didn't make it." She hung her head. "I'm sorry, Irene.

I know he was a friend of yours, but he was a thug, too. It's always just a matter of time before guys like him get back what they've been giving." he said in his cop voice. "He was good to me before Jackie was born, and no matter what he was or wasn't, I can't ever forget that. Well, I guess I had better get going, I'm leaving again in the morning." Can I drive you to your hotel? We'll make one quick drive down Corrine and Marconi if you want," he offered. Sure, why not?" With that she got up to say goodbye to Mikey. She hugged him and said she would be seeing him. Don't make it so long next time! I miss you around here," he smiled as she hugged him.

As they were driving around, she couldn't resist asking, "Have you seen Curly around?" "Nah, Curly disappeared about the time you left. Nobody's seen him since. We all kind of thought you two ran off on that yacht of his! Its been missing, too," he said smiling. "No, it never worked out for us, I guess it just wasn't meant to be." "You married or seeing anyone?" he questioned. "No, once you've had steak it's hard to settle for hamburger!" she said with a wink. They laughed as they were getting out of the car at her hotel. They hugged, "Good to see you, Irene. Take care of yourself and tell Jackie hello." "I will, Jock. Be good to yourself. I'll be seeing you." With that she closed the door. The next day she went back to Winter Haven, with the unmistakable knowledge that her life with Curly was truly dead and nothing could bring it back no matter how much she wanted it.

Jackie was beginning to miss her mother. She was not running from her, in fact she had come to realize she was not running from anything. Instead, she was running toward something, her independence and slaying the dragons that haunted her. She had conquered both, somewhat.

Working with the Barretts had afforded Jackie opportunities she would not have had otherwise. For instance, she was invited to tour with the Bob Hope Christmas Show, but because it was in Vietnam, and she was underage, she couldn't go. The Barretts did not have legal custody of Jackie, and the red tape would have been such a hassle, it made it impossible for her to go. She was so young and the risk was too great for the Barretts to chance getting caught exploiting this child.

During the off–season Jackie went to Winter Haven to be with her mother. They spent a great deal of quality time together. Jackie didn't discuss her job with her mother; she knew Irene would not approve of her dancing naked in front of people! Irene didn't ask questions about what she did, which made Jackie suspicious she already knew about it.

Lonnie contacted Jackie about being an escort for one of the celebrities that would be attending the New Years Eve bash at the Sportsman's Club, an exclusive club for moneyed people. The owners of different carnivals such as J.E. Straits, Dell and Trevor, and Roll America, along with prominent invited guests attended this function every year.

Jackie was proud to be invited to this affair, and accepted wholeheartedly. Lonnie told her to wear her emerald green dress, fix her hair and make–up pretty. He would send a car for her.

Several of the girls from the show were working the party, too. Lonnie assigned each girl a table. When the guests arrived the girl hosting that guest would greet them at the car and escort him to the table. They would dance with the guest, get drinks for them, whatever they needed, the hostess saw they received it. Jackie was hostess to one of the world's most famous men, Walt Disney.

He was a kind gentleman and treated Jackie with the utmost respect. The girls had been told to let the guest do the talking, not to interrupt the conversations, and not to ask for autographs.

Mr. Disney was interested in Jackie. He asked her name, "Jackie, Sir." she answered respectably. I'm Walt Disney, he replied.

Their conversation continued as he asked her what she planned to be when she grew up. He commented on what a beautiful young girl she was and if she would agree, he would send her to a finishing school in Paris, France to make a real lady of her. She thanked him for his interest, someone else began talking with him and she had to let their conversation go.

She wondered if the other girls were getting offers like hers. She wished she could go to Paris, France to school, but she knew it would never happen. "At least someone offered me the chance!" she said to herself sadly.

The clock struck twelve, the orchestra began playing Auld Lang Syne, everyone was yelling "Happy New Year", throwing confetti, and kissing each other. Mr. Disney hugged her and kissed her on the forehead in a fatherly fashion. She would never forget his kindness or his generous offer. When she escorted him back to his car he said, "Thank you for a most enjoyable evening, Jacqueline." Then he closed the door, waving as the car pulled away. As Jackie was waving she wondered how he knew her whole name. She shrugged her shoulders and went inside.

CHAPTER THIRTEEN

In the spring Irene, Jackie, Gus, Cal, and Billy re–joined the Straits carnival for another season. Irene had opened two new shows in one large trailer billed as the 'Torture Rama'. The shows were called the 'Headless Madonna' and 'The Tiniest Mermaid'. The last time Jackie was with the carnival she met Wendy, a young girl about her age. She came to work for Irene. Wendy agreed to come to work for Irene, taking turns with Jackie as the 'Tiniest Mermaid' and the 'Headless Madonna'. It felt good to be around someone her own age for a change, and to be doing something besides stripping. The shows were very tiresome, however and the girls had to take frequent breaks. During their breaks they would meet behind the trailer and smoke, when time permitted they would go to their favorite rides and talk the ride jockeys into letting them ride.

One day a new ride was being constructed next to the Torture Rama, the octopus. This was the first time the ride had been featured in America. Along with the new ride came two new ride jockeys. Jackie and Wendy were very interested in both. For two days they watched as the guys put the finishing touches on the ride. Wendy picked out the longhaired, blonde, bearded guy to flirt with, Jackie chose the dark haired, pencil thin mustached, tattooed one. Once the ride was completed the girls walked over to inspect it and the ride jockeys.

"What's this called?" Jackie asked as she ran her hand over the railing. "The octopus, it's new, first time it's been in the U.S.," the dark haired one answered. "Does it go fast", Wendy asked. "Pretty fast. I guess it's about the fastest, except for the roller coasters," the blonde one remarked. "It's a smooth ride, kind of glides. Here get in and judge for yourself!" the dark haired one said as he opened the gate. Jackie jumped in and as it began to move the boy jumped in with her. They rode for fifteen minutes. Jackie loved the feel of the ride, and she enjoyed sitting with him. When the ride was over, he introduced himself. "I'm Rob," he said as he wiped his hand on his jeans and sticking it out to her. "I'm Jackie", she answered demurely, with her head bowed as he took her hand. Wendy and the other jockey were having their own conversation. Jackie couldn't believe how much better looking Rob was up close, with his raven hair, brown eyes, and dark complexion. She could tell from the trailer he had tattoos, up close she recognized Lassie, an eagle, and a dancing girl. "I like your tattoos." she said. "Thanks, this one dances!" he said as he flexed his muscle.

She liked the way the girl danced when he moved his arm! She took her fingers and felt of the tattoo as he flexed his arm. She liked the feel of his muscle and his skin.

Her newfound friend invited her out for dinner, which in carnival life was going to a grab joint for a Polish sausage and riding the rides. When the ride closed for the night, Rob took Jackie to a bar in town. Jackie was too young to be served liquor, but Rob was of age to drink. She would have a soft drink and he a beer. This same scenario took place several nights that week. One night, rain closed the carnival early, Jackie and Rob made plans to go into town, as they were leaving he leaned her against the truck, kissed her, and whispered in her ear, "How would you like to meet your father?" Jackie was taken aback, then gathering her wits laughed aloud and said, "What are you talking about? How do you know him?" She had always kept the image of him leaning against his car at the service station in the back of her mind. She had brought the memory to life when she was scared or had self–doubt. Now, here was a man standing before her asking if she wanted to meet him! Rob told her if she did, she would have to listen to what he had to tell her, and follow his directions. She agreed to listen. He told her she could not tell anyone, not even her mother or Wendy or it would not happen. Rob explained that people would need to believe they were in love, a couple. He told her he was a married man with a little son, and that he was sent by her father to bring her to him if she wanted to come. He was sorry to lead her on, but he had to gain her confidence, that was how he was told to do it. Jackie was disappointed their relationship couldn't grow into something more. She thought about what he was proposing and decided she had to take a chance and trust him. She wanted to meet her father; she had a million questions to ask him! She agreed to his terms.

Rob and Jackie were together for two carnival spots. After the show closed they went to Irene and told her they wanted to live together. They wanted to find work with another carnival. Irene knew she could not stop Jackie from pursuing young love. She remembered how she stowed away on a yacht to pursue her one and only true love. She told Jackie she wouldn't stand in her way.

They went to Broward County and Miami, then to Largo. Jackie was getting anxious to see her father, but Rob told her they had to be careful. Too many eyes and ears were on her, always had been. He told her she didn't understand what they were dealing with, that her safety as well as her father's had to be paramount to anything else, including her wants. For the plan to work, people had to see them as a normal couple with nothing on their minds but work and play. There could be no hint of a meeting of any kind, and if she became too anxious, the deal would be off. She knew he was serious and she would never mention it again! He had convinced her that she could trust him and depend on him. She would just have to wait.

Rob told her to pack up and wait for him at the main gate while he collected their pay and found them a ride. Jackie obeyed.

Several years earlier Gus had given Jackie a white German shepherd puppy, which she named Champaign. It was now full grown. Although Rob was calling the shots in this operation, her only condition was that Champaign would not be left behind. She and Champaign were waiting for Rob by the gate when Bonanza stars Lorne Greene, Dan Blocker, and Michael Landon came in. They were appearing as the main attraction on the grandstand. The three stopped to pet Champaign and talk with Jackie for a minute, and then went on their way. She was so excited to meet such famous people! She had a great deal of childlike enthusiasm, as her childhood had been severed when she entered carnival life.

Rob got them a ride with another carnie who was going as far as Tampa. He knew Jackie and Champaign and was glad to have the company. Once in Tampa the rides became harder to acquire. Rob would go to a bar and scope out car tags for rides to places on their schedule. Then he would go inside, find out the owner of the car, and offer them a few bucks to let them ride. Sometimes it worked if the guy wasn't afraid of Champaign. Sometimes they would just drive off before Rob could load himself, Jackie, and Champaign into the car or truck. Big riggers were kind and when they could find a truck stop they would generally find someone who would let Champaign ride in the trailer, (if they weren't carrying edibles), Jackie and Rob would ride in the cab.

They traveled north and when they could find a fair or carnival they would work a week or so. Rob kept reminding her that they had to look like they were traveling to work, not to escape. They also had to eat, as did the dog!

When they finally got to New York, they rented a motel room for a week while they prepared to leave the country. Jackie and Rob were required to get tetanus and booster shots; Champaign had to have all his shots updated as well.

As they boarded the train, Champaign was taken to the animal car and would remain there for the remainder of the trip.

They talked for awhile, but unlike Rob, Jackie was too excited and nervous to sleep. Too many questions without answers were gnawing at her minds eye. What do you say to someone who should have been with you for the past sixteen years, but didn't find you necessary until now? Why was 'he' sending for her now? Why all the mystery? This kind of mystery was the reason she was afraid of him. Her mother never talked about her father. He just never seemed to come up in conversation. She didn't even know his name! She had always known when her mother and granny were talking about him, because they referred to him as 'he' or 'him'. There were so many questions Jackie wanted to ask her mother about 'him', but it seemed every time she decided to ask, something happened regarding 'him' to upset her mother, so she didn't ask. 'He' became unimportant when they entered the carnival and she didn't want to bring 'him' up. Jackie remembered times she had seen the damage 'he' had done or caused her mother physically, mentally, and emotionally. Although her mother was no saint, she didn't deserve the treatment she had received from 'him' over the years. She wanted him to justify every tear 'he' caused her mother....and her!

CHAPTER FOURTEEN

"Last stop before Ontario, Canada", the conductor yelled. The sound of metal wheels screeching across metal tracks as the brakes squealed to a stop made Jackie's skin crawl. What secrets was she to learn from 'him'? Would she still hate 'him' for abandoning her and her mother? How was she suppose to act, dress, speak? What does one say to the person that gave them life and then…took away her childhood? What could she say to the man that could have given her and her mother a decent life, without them having to all but pimp themselves out in carnival life? How do you force yourself to be cordial to a man that now wants to call himself 'Daddy', when he has never shown he even knows the meaning of the word? She began to feel doubtful about all this when the train whistle blew and snapped her back to the present. She could feel her face had turned red, (a trait she would soon learn she had inherited from 'him', along with her eye color, complexion, and the ability to curl her lip).

She wasn't sure she was ready to face this demon, the giver of her life, the destroyer of her childhood.

The jolt of the train awakened Rob. Jackie asked, "What happens next?" Rob was reluctant to discuss details. "You've waited this long, now it will be just a little longer,", he said softly as he patted her on the head. "What's he like? she asked. "You'll have to form your own opinions and judgments. I don't know him all that well. He's always been nice enough, to me," he informed her.

"Yeah, well I have already formed my opinions about him, and most of them are bad. I really don't know why I agreed to this. I guess I was curious," she remarked. "It's not too late to back out, you know?" He said rather provoked. "I'm sorry, Rob I don't mean to sound like it's your fault or that I don't appreciate what you have done. It's just he has not ever been a part of my life and this is all weird to me. That's all," she said pouting. "I understand. I can't say I know how you feel, but maybe you should give him a chance to explain." "How can he just explain me away, Rob?", she asked. He shook his head and answered, "I don't know, Jackie. It's just that you might always regret it if you don't see him." "I know your right, I just don't know what to say to him, it's awkward."

Rob changed the subject, hoping she wouldn't change her mind about meeting her father. He asked her about her life in the carnival. She told him about the shows her mother had and the snake pit. She left out the strip shows. She told him about riding in the famous Gasporilla Parade in a dragon car and meeting Walt Disney. Then she asked about him, he said there wasn't much to tell and he laid his head back, she followed his lead. No more questions were asked.

When the train screeched and squealed to the final stop, she couldn't make her feet move! Rob took her hand and grabbed their brown paper bag luggage. Her feet began to shuffle off the train. The thoughts of having to hitch another ride made her stomach churn. The wind was so cold it chilled her to the bone. She was upset when she learned Champaign would be in quarantine for ten days! She was angry she couldn't even see him. Rob assured her he would be well taken care of, it was just the law and it had to be obeyed. A man driving a checkered car offered them a ride. When the driver asked, "Where to?", Rob shoved a piece of paper with the address over the seat. When the driver had looked at it, he handed it back to Rob and he destroyed the paper.

They rode only a few minutes before turning onto a long drive lined with the largest pine trees Jackie had ever seen. She could hear the large cones being crushed as they drove over them. At the end of the drive was a small white–framed house with green shutters and door. She couldn't help wondering what awaited her behind that door. As the cab approached the house, Jackie thought they would be stopping in the front, but just as the driver applied the brakes, Rob leaned over the seat and told the driver to pull around to the back. Rob apparently noticed the look on Jackie's face and realized going around to the back had made her feel she wasn't good enough to use the front entrance! "Mother will probably be in the kitchen cooking dinner. I wanted to surprise her," he explained. Jackie breathed a sigh of relief and managed a smile.

As they piled out of the cab she could hear an animal howling in the distance, it was an eerie sound; she hoped it was not beckoning her to go home.

As her feet crunched the new fallen snow, she realized just how cold she really was, yet she knew her coldness was not completely from the lack of heat outside, but from the lack of warmth she felt for 'him' inside. She was determined to show 'him' he did not deserve her love, respect, or even her fear! It was 'curiosity' that brought her here, nothing else.

She could see through the window as she walked up the back steps to the small porch. The lady standing at the sink had gray curly hair, and was neatly dressed. Rob rapped lightly on the door; she turned to see them. The look of excitement when she saw Rob let Jackie know she was his mother, and that she was glad he had come. Apparently, it had been quite some time since she had seen him. When she opened the door Rob grabbed her and swung her around the kitchen like Jackie had done the life–sized doll she received mysteriously one Christmas. When he put her down, he introduced Jackie. "You look just like your father!" she said as she gave Jackie a hug. "I'm Lillian. I'm glad you have come, your father needs to see you now.", she said. Jackie wasn't at all sure what she meant by that statement, but she wanted to respond with, "Yeah, well I've needed to see 'him' a lot of times in my life and 'he' didn't come, so let's go Rob, I've changed my mind," but, somehow she couldn't. She just had to know what this was all about and why he had just forgotten about her and her mother. Besides, if 'he' was so anxious to see her now, why wasn't 'he' here to greet her?!

Lillian had cooked a huge pot of stew and fresh bread. It was delicious and warm. They were happy to be eating something besides gooey peanut butter and jelly on stale bread.

As Jackie was putting her bowl in the sink, she could see down a dark hallway, at the end was a door with a light streaming beneath it. She just knew 'he' was behind that door, and she knew when it opened, her life would never be the same. She was uncertain as to whether it would be better or worse, but she was certain it would definitely change!

She cleared her throat and conjured up enough courage to ask if 'he' was in that room?

"Yes, dear, he is, but you can't go in just now," Lillian answered. She slowly took her seat back at the table. She had a million and one questions she would have asked her, but somehow she knew she wouldn't tell her the answers. Besides, she really wanted to hear the answers from 'him', after all, 'he' was the reason she was there.

Rob and Lillian were enjoying their visit. Jackie was dying to get a look at the rest of the house, so she asked where the bathroom was. To her disappointment it was just off the kitchen! As she was closing the bathroom door she heard a man's voice from the other room. She hurried as quickly as possible, washed her hands and re–entered the kitchen. Rob was sitting at the table alone. "Where is Lillian?" she whispered. "She was summoned to the bedroom," Rob replied. Then, Lillian called for Rob to come to the bedroom. "My turn," he said. with a chuckle. Jackie's heart began to skip beats. She just knew when they came out; she would be summoned in! She was right! Lillian came back to the kitchen, "He wants to see you, now." Lillian led her into the dark hallway and motioned for her to sit on a wicker–seated latter back chair. Then she opened the curtain in the dining room to give a little light in the hallway, and walked back into the kitchen. Jackie placed her feet on the rungs of the chair so her legs wouldn't shake. She folded her hands so tightly her knuckles turned white. Once again she felt her face flush. She had no idea what she would say to 'him' when she finally saw him. A small stream of light shown on the walls, just enough to illuminate dusty pictures hanging in arranged order. She thought how funny it was to watch dust particles floating in the air when sunlight was shining directly on the glass. She wondered why you could only see that when a small stream of light was bouncing off glass. She tried to think of anything other than going into that room! She wanted to get up from the chair, but she just couldn't make her feet move off the rung. She slid forward enough to escape the glare of the blinding sunlight, so she could see the people in the pictures. She recognized the men as the Three Stooges, as she continued to stare at the chubby, bald one, her mouth dropped opened. It was 'him'! She recognized him as the man leaning against the car at the service station!

The door opened slowly, Rob came out and said goodbye, "I'll see you soon," he hugged her and left. As the light of the room flooded the hall-way, there in front of her stood a man whose frail frame revealed the larger man he had once been, but sill the same man who had abandoned her years earlier, the man in the picture!

They stood there just staring at one another for what seemed to Jackie an hour, but in reality was only a few seconds. Finally, 'he' broke the long awaited silence, in a strong, but rather raspy voice he announced, "Jacqueline, I'm your Pop." She stood there for a second and proclaimed, "Hey, I know you! You're a Stooge!" He smiled, "I can't believe you said that! That's exactly what your mama said to me the first time she met me."

Jackie stood there not really knowing what he expected her to say or do. She had mixed emotions, part of her wanted to run to him, throw her arms around him like she would pretend she did when she was little. The other part of her wanted to flog him, hit him, bite him, hurt him like he had hurt her and her mother. She was afraid if she moved she would do the latter! She continued to stand there with a blank look on her face. Finally, he said, "Won't you come sit for awhile?" He ushered her into his room and she sat on a chair near his bed, he sat on the side of his bed.

His room was nothing special, very plainly decorated and furnished with an old iron bed, a dresser with a mirror, a night table, and the chair, (much like the one in the hall). There was no television or radio. An alarm clock, a lamp, medicine bottles and a half full glass of water cluttered the night table. There was a multicolored woven rug covering the hardwood floor beside the bed. His brown leather house shoes rested on the rug. He hung his olive green terry cloth robe over the foot of his bed. He was very meticulous with the arranging of his belongings. Jackie watched as he got comfortable. "I'm glad you decided to come." he remarked. "I gave it a lot of thought; I almost didn't come", she replied. "What changed your mind?" "I was curious", she said as she got out of the chair to examine the contents on his dresser. As she picked up his gold watch she said, "I wanted to see how the other half lived," she watched his expression from the mirror. He dropped his head, "Are you disappointed?" "Yeah, I was expecting you to be living high on the hog!" she said with a sting. "I'm sorry, I don't follow what you mean." "Really? I mean you never spent any of your money on me or my mother, so I figured you must be spending it on something or maybe someone." I understand your bitterness, Jacqueline, but I was in hopes we could get passed all that and try to develop a respectful relationship." "I'll bet you were! Your damn right I'm bitter…"Pop" was it? Yeah I'm bitter, and as for the respect thing, don't count on it!" "I would prefer you conduct yourself as a lady. Cursing cheapens a woman." "Um…how about tattoos, do they make a woman a lady or do they cheapen her?" He knew she was referring to Irene's tattoos, that opened the door for him to ask, "How is your mother?" "Oh, she's just hunky dory! What do you care?" "I know you probably won't believe me, right now, but I really loved your mother and you. Sometimes, Jacqueline, things happen that we have no control over." She interrupted, "Yeah, like having babies you don't take care of and…",he interrupted her, "No! Like things I will try to explain while you are here if you can settle down some and let me. Your feisty like your mother, and for the most part that's not a bad thing," he chuckled. "What's not bad, being feisty or being like my mother? I don't really like you talking about her." "Well, it's getting late why don't you let Lillian show you around and get you settled in. We'll have plenty of time to talk and catch up." "You sure? Are you sick or just really old and stuff?" "Both I'm afraid," he called for Lillian. "Goodnight, Jacqueline." "Not really," she replied.

Lillian escorted her through the house showing her where to put her things. "It's a good thing I don't have much! This is the first time not having much has come in handy." Lillian pretended not to hear her, but Jackie knew she did. "What's your story, Lillian? I mean besides being Rob's mother. Are you 'his' nurse or what?" she asked rather belligerently. "I'm his…" her voice trailed. Jackie's heart jumped into her throat. She had never thought about 'him' having a wife besides her mother! Maybe this was the answer. "How long have you been with him?" she asked. "Oh, about three years, now. I was his nurse and he needed me when he came home from the hospital. My job wouldn't permit me to nurse him and work too, so I chose to be with him. He's really not a bad person, Jacqueline you should give him a chance." "Well, Lillian, you've only known him for three or four years, people change when they get old, about to die. His wife, my mother, was an authority on 'him' and I hid in the shadows when she would cry to my Granny because of 'him' so Lillian, he really has been a 'bad' person, and he's had seventeen years to take this chance. I refuse to feel sorry for him, I'd have to respect him to do that, and I don't; probably never will. I'm not here for him. Thanks for the tour, can I please get ready for bed now?" Lillian gave her a towel and wash cloth so she could shower before going to bed. I don't have pajamas or a gown," she said. "Oh, I picked up a few things for you. Your father told Rob not to bring a lot of things with you. I hope they fit." "Thanks, Lillian, I'm sure they will fit fine"; they did. As she showered she thought how 'empty' the house was, not just the feeling, but there was nothing that made it look like a home. That one picture was the only one in the entire house! There were no books, except the Bible on his dresser. She wondered if he were a celebrity why he didn't have his house furnished better, and have anything that looked like he lived there for real.

After she showered and dressed she went to the dining room where she was to sleep on a fold out couch. She fell asleep almost as soon as she laid her head on the pillow. It was morning before she knew it. The smell of bacon awoke her. She wanted to bound out of bed and run to the delicious smell, but her anger and pride stopped her. She didn't want to appear too anxious to be around 'him', so she lay back down. A few minutes later Lillian came in, "Jacqueline, breakfast is ready. Your father will wait for you to wash up," she said. She walked back into the kitchen, Jackie got up. While she was in the bathroom she thought about what she would say when she got to the table. She couldn't think of anything she thought would really annoy 'him', so she decided to take her time before going to the kitchen. She was surprised to find Lillian getting her coat and gloves on, "I have to go to the market, is there anything special you would like?" "I'm not too picky. I like just about anything, but my favorite is hamburgers and French fries," she said smiling. "You sound just like your father, he could eat hamburgers at every meal!" She laughed slightly. Jackie made no comment. "He's in the living room if you want to join him. I'll be back soon," she closed the door behind her. Jackie didn't know how to approach him so she sat at the table until she finished her breakfast. Then she washed her plate and fork. As she stood at the sink he came into the kitchen for a refill of coffee. "Good morning," he said cheerfully. "Did you sleep well?" "Yeah, I was tired," she answered. as she dried her hands and headed back into the dining room. "I'm watching television in the living room if you would like to join me," he invited. Without a word she followed him. She was shocked that he was watching Bugs Bunny! He was one of her favorites. "Do you like Bugs Bunny?" he asked. She thought, "Had he been around when I was little he would know whether or not I liked Bugs Bunny!" "It's a little late to be wondering if I like Bugs Bunny or not, don't you think? Did you ever wonder that, when I was little, or is it just now crossing your mind?" "I've wondered about a great many things concerning you, Jacqueline. I can't honestly say I ever wondered about your feelings for Bugs Bunny. However, I did think about you," he replied. "You could have lied and said,'yes'. It would have been nice to think you wondered those things," she said. in a pouting tone. "I will do many things, Jacqueline, but I will not lie to you." "Whew! What a relief! I wondered if you were honest or not. Since you are being so honest, tell me why everybody around here calls me by my whole name? I'm used to hearing it only when I've been bad, or I'm being introduced to someone," she said. "Do you prefer another name?" "I didn't say that, I asked you why you call me the whole thing?" "I named you after a good friend's little girl." Yeah, I know all about that. Do you have my name tattooed on your arm, too?" "No, I don't have any tattoos." "I'm surprised, you sure made sure my Mama had plenty! What was that about anyway?" she inquired. "Well, some things are hard to explain to others. They all had a special significance, like memorable years. The one across her back is self explanatory, and our favorite cuisine was Chinese food, 'sweet and sour' pork and chicken. It probably doesn't sound very romantic to you, but I really didn't do it for meanness or torture. How did you know I had anything to do with Irene's tattoos?" "I used to hear Mama and Granny talking when they thought I was asleep," he chuckled. "It's not funny!" she said wrinkling her eyebrows and half laughing. "I spent most of my childhood eaves dropping on my Mama and Granny just to hear something about you!" He laughed, "I'm honored that you were that interested!" "I saw you once, you know?" "I remember. I had come by to see you and your Mama before Christmas. I watched you sleeping. You looked just like an angel lying there. I kissed you on the cheek and whispered for you to look for me the next morning at the service station. Remember I waved at you?" "At first I thought I had dreamed it. That must be what Granny meant when she said that our dreams do have meanings, she knew you were there the night before. I always thought of you standing against that car. Since I didn't really know anything about you, I would pretend you had some real important job and were out of the country. I was told by someone, maybe Aunt Alice, that you were an ambassador."

"I'm sorry to disappoint you, but you did get the 'out of the country' part correct." They both laughed. Jackie found herself warming up to him. She wasn't sure she wanted to get too friendly, she was afraid of being hurt. She excused herself to help Lillian get the groceries in and put them away.

For most of her stay, Lillian would make herself scarce, so that Jackie could spend private time with her father. He had promised to answer any questions she had, but somehow now that she had the opportunity she couldn't think of any. She was hoping he would begin at the beginning and tell her all about her mother and him. All she knew was bits and pieces she had heard eaves dropping. She asked, "Will you tell me about you and Mama? When you first met and all?" "Didn't your Mother ever tell you about me, our wedding, or anything?" he said in an unbelievable tone. "No, I never asked her because she was so sad or scared every time she talked to Granny about you. Granny told me once that I shouldn't bother Mama about my father, so I didn't. The only time I remember ever mentioning you was when I asked Mama why you didn't live with us, Granny hushed me up and said when Mama thought I was old enough to understand she would tell me what I needed to know. I guess she still doesn't think I'm old enough, because she has never mentioned you to me. Will you tell me, please?" she begged.

"Well, let me say that I am the reason she never told you anything about me. I asked her not to because I wanted to tell you someday myself. I am glad she kept her promise to me, but I am sorry it caused you so much pain. I first met your Mama when she was just thirteen...." He continued to tell her about their first meeting, California, Cal and Gus's trial, their elopement, her birth. He told her most of the good and some of the bad about their relationship. They laughed and cried for hours. Then he shuffled to his dresser, took out a man's yellowed handkerchief, with the letter 'C' monogrammed on it and handed it to her. She could tell there was something wrapped inside. She unfolded the handkerchief and one dingy white lace glove fell onto her lap. "What's this?" she asked "It's your Mother's glove, I picked it up at the trial, remember?" "Oh, the one she dropped when you were at Uncle Cal's and Uncle Gus's trial. As she held the glove in her hand she thought about how much he must have loved her Mother to have kept something this insignificant. For the first time she saw the side of him her Mother must have fallen in love with. Now she felt a connection with both her parents, and it amazed her that the peace she had longed for all her life was handed to her wrapped in a tear–stained handkerchief! As she handed it back to him, she saw him put it to his lips, close his eyes, and kiss it. Then he gently wrapped it back in the handkerchief and put it away. She got up to leave him with his memories, as she was leaving he said with tears in his eyes, "I'll see to that you get this some-day." Without a word she went to bed , where she cried herself to sleep.

Chapter Fifteen

Their visit the next day began with a hearty breakfast and cartoons. Lillian left again.

"I'll try to tell you everything before you leave. I want you to know the truth about a great many things, Jacqueline. There are things you need to know now and things that will not become important until you are much older. Many things have happened, but many things you need to know about have not yet come to pass. Some of what I will tell you will seem like riddles, but as time goes by you will be able to solve the puzzle. There are people who can help you, Jacqueline, but you will not be able to contact them until after my real death. There are things I will tell you that can place you in a great deal of danger until after my death. After I die you will probably be safe. I don't want to tell you everything at once. It is a lot to comprehend. I have written a book that is based on certain aspects of my life. I changed the names to protect you and your mother. I'll tell you more about that later, too. What I have said all of this for, is to ask you to please not shut me out. I know I have no right to ask anything of you, but I need you to know these things. Your mother doesn't know a lot about me, Jacqueline. She loved the man I always wanted to be and could only be when we were together. She brought that man out of me when nobody could. She saw my soul and my heart. You know, I was much older than her. She made me feel young and alive, important. Not because of my career, hell it was nearly over when I met her, but because she loved me. I could be my real self with her. When I would have to leave her it would nearly kill me, I know it hurt her, too. No matter what you might think of me, Jacqueline I want you to believe me when I tell you that I have loved

133

your mother since the first day I laid eyes on her, and I have loved you from the minute I knew you were going to be!" "Then why did you do mean things to her?" "What are you talking about? I was never mean to her, I loved her," he retorted. "You didn't think it was mean when you told those men to wring her breasts in the wringer washing machine?" she snapped. "I didn't have a damn thing to do with that!" he snapped. I knew nothing about it until later. I had been to see you a few days before and decided I would have them take you to be with my Mother for awhile, hoping after she saw you it might make a difference to my family and we could all be together. I took my camera because I wanted a picture of you. I left without the camera and I told the three idiots I sent for you to get it. It wasn't until the pictures were developed that I saw what they had done! Let me assure you one of them will never bother another lady or anyone else, because I killed him with my bare hands!" he said profoundly. "Did you really kill him or were you just saying that?" she questioned doubt-fully. I would never just tell you something to be saying it! If I tell you, it is the truth. Otherwise, when I die you will have nothing I intended for you to have. It is with a great deal of remorse that I had to end certain people's lives, as an order from my family, but that son of a bitch I enjoyed killing and have never felt bad about it one time. I would have killed him twice if it would have caused him anymore pain! I also killed another man for bothering your mother. I would not have stood for her to be hurt by anybody!" he exclaimed. "What about the other two men that hurt mama with that washing machine? Did you kill them, too?" The other ones will sing soprano for the rest of their lives!" he explained. "Huh? What does that mean?' He laughed, 'It's an expression. They hurt because of it, that's all." "What happened to the pictures?" "I destroyed them, but they claimed the negatives were ruined at the photo lab. The one that had the pictures, damn well better pray they never surface, because if they do, he won't. I'll see to it.

I swear to you that there has never been one day of your life that I haven't thought about you, wished you and your mother were with me, and cried because you weren't." Tears were streaming down her face, he was crying too. When she realized he was crying she wanted to go to him and put her arms around his waist so they could hold each other while they cried, but she didn't.

Later, she asked him how long he had been in Canada, and why he couldn't have brought her and her mother with him. I was brought here for protection and was advised by Hoover not to. Since he was calling the shots I felt it was in everybody's best interest not to rock the boat". He didn't answer her question about how long he had been there, and she didn't pursue it because she knew it must be top secret.

Is that why you stay here, in this…little house? You know, it looks as if You really don't live here," she observed. "I didn't tell you I lived here. You assumed I did because this is where I am and we eat and sleep here. Things are not always what they seem, Jacqueline. You should learn that at an early age. Question things, that's how you learn. That is what will help you in your search for the truth." he said. "Well, do you live here?" she asked again. He did not answer her, he smiled, shrugged and walked into the livingroom turning on the television. The only 'homey' looking thing in the house.

Rob had not been back to the house since he dropped Champaign off two weeks before. Jackie overheard Lillian telling her father that she had lunch with him and his family, and how much the baby had grown. Jackie was glad she had not been present for that conversation, so they could not see the sick feeling on her face. She really cared for Rob, and it hurt that he could never feel the same for her. She was tired of her life being pretend! She thought about how she had made up in her mind about her father. Now, she had to pretend an out and out lie just to meet him! It seemed as if every time she thought she could like 'him' something happened or she would have a thought that would make her remember her hate for him! She wondered if she would ever get passed the feelings of abandonment and resentment she felt for 'him'. Maybe she would learn something that would magically cause all the bad, hurtful, resentful feelings to disappear.

She wanted more than anything else to understand why he had been absent from her life for so long.

Lillian seemed to make herself scarce for longer periods now. Jackie knew it was so she and her father could be alone, but she wasn't sure if he had told her to leave or if she just did it on her own. In a way she was glad to finally have the opportunity to be with him and have his undivided attention. She decided to make an effort to get along with him, after all what did she have to loose?

"Did your Mother ever tell you she stowed away on my yacht just to be with me?" "No! Did she really?" He laughed as he recounted the story. She smiled as he told it. She could just see her Mama! She wondered what in the world would cause someone to leave somebody they obviously adored, and who idealized and loved them. She didn't have the courage to ask him, she hoped he would explain on his own.

"I wish things could have been different for Irene and me. She deserved better, so did you. I loved that woman so much I ached for her at times! Still do. I loved her and you too much to take a chance on something happening because of me. You see, Jacqueline, as you well know, we don't get to choose the families we are born into." He smiled and shook his head, I had this same conversation with your mama. It seems like yesterday in a way, and yet it seems like I read it somewhere or something, like it never really happened. Anyway, I was from a family that had come to the United States from Sicily, and they don't consider themselves bound by the laws of the land, any land. They have their own laws and although many hated them; everyone revered them. They expected loyalty from their members and would accept nothing less. When people disobeyed, refused, or tattled on them they ended up dead, or worse, someone they loved. Do you remember Joe Allums?" "Uncle Joe? Yes, why?" "Well, he came to live with my family when he was about ten years old. His father had worked for my Grandfather and he turned on my family, so they killed Joe's mother and father. They took Joe in and made him part of our family out of respect for his 'poor dead mother'." "But, she wouldn't have been dead if they hadn't killed her!" she snapped. "I know, but that is the way it works in a family like mine. Do you remember when your mother took you to Jacksonville?" "Yes, it was awful! We ate bologna for a month! Why? How did you know about that?" "That was the first and last time in all the time I have known Irene that I didn't know where she was and what she was doing! My family was mad as hell because she called the police to identify the body of a woman that had talked too much about the family's business." Jackie interrupted, "Edie! That was Edie! You mean they…your family killed Edie!?" "I mean your mother tattled and that caused a bad thing to happen. Why did you have to leave Jacksonville, do you remember?" "Yes, because Mama's sister, Aunt Marie was…murdered, just like Edie…" her voice trailed. Now do you understand what I've been saying? I had no choice where your mother and I were concerned. You see, my marrying her in the first place broke two family rules. Your Uncle Cal worked for another family like mine in Tampa. Therefore, my family thought your mother couldn't be trusted. Then, my family was Catholic and your mother wasn't. When we eloped, it made my family very upset because we were not married by a Priest, and because your mother wasn't Catholic. While we were on our honeymoon cruise for three months they had our marriage annulled. Had I gone against them and remarried her, they would have killed you, or your grandmother or your mother, just to hurt me. I couldn't risk it. I just couldn't. It would have been my signing a death warrant for people I loved! I tried to explain all of this to your mother. I know it was hard for her to understand, as I am sure it is for you. I just had to tell you so you would know why things were the way they were. I was supposed to be next in line to run the family when my Uncle died. I didn't want any part of it. It had destroyed the only thing in life that meant anything to me; my marriage and family. So when Uncle Guido died I told Edgar everything about Trafficani, Marcello, and the others that were important to his investigations. I knew another family would kill me as soon as I took over, so I got out. There are some things I need to tell you, that will be important for you to know, but right now I'm too tired. We'll talk more later," he whispered.

Lillian came in to fix dinner. Jackie and her father went into the living room to watch television. "Have you ever watched Roller Derby?" he asked. "I've seen it once or twice, I really don't understand it much." He began to explain it to her. Before she knew it she was rooting against his favorite! When he thought she wasn't looking, he watched her enthusiasm, realizing how much he had missed. She saw him watching and realized she had missed a lot not having him around when she was growing up. It was a learning experience for both.

ƒ

CHAPTER SIXTEEN

The next morning Lillian left early. She had fixed breakfast for the two of them. As they were eating he said, "How old were you when President Kennedy died, seven, eight or nine?" "Yeah, I think so," she mumbled. with her mouth full. "Did you know he came to your house the day before he died?" "I was there! I came in from school and he was on the porch with Granny!" "What did your Mama tell you about him coming to your house?" he asked. "She didn't tell me, I told her. She was at work when he came. Granny said he was there about Uncle Cal." At the mention of Cal's name he gritted his teeth and made a roaring sound. She got the feeling he didn't care for Cal. She laughed, "Why are you growling? Don't you like Uncle Cal?" she teased. He stopped gritting and growling and said, "That's another story let's get through this one first." He smiled, took a deep breath, "The early sixties were a very turbulent time, Jacqueline. There was trouble among blacks and whites, the KKK was fighting against the blacks receiving their Civil Rights, racial riots were happening in every city across America, especially the south, and Tampa was no exception. Around sixty one, John Kennedy's brother, Robert who had been made Attorney General when John took office was nosing around trying to expose organized crime, which was families like mine, Trafficani, Marcello, and there were other ones, too many to tell you about, but just so you get the picture," he looked at her as if asking a question. "I get it, go on. Why was he at our house?" "Well, the Kennedy's didn't like old Edgar; hell everybody hates him to some degree because he blackmails everybody! Anyway, John got word that there was a plot among the mob families to assassinate Fidel Castro in Cuba. He knew there had been gun running from Tampa to

Cuba, he figured Edgar was involved and he wanted to talk to Cal because he was in with Trafficani's bunch. Your Uncle Cal (he said gritting his teeth and growling his name), worked on the shrimp boats that ran for the mob. They were doing more on those boats than catching shrimp. They ran to Cuba trading weapons for cigars and dope. If they had to get anybody out of the way, they used the shrimp boats to dump the bodies in the ocean, deep enough that they had no chance of surfacing. Kennedy wanted to know what he knew about what was going on, but Cal (grit and growl) was in jail when he came to Tampa. Kennedy was also asking about me because of my family ties. The Kennedy's hated Edgar and he hated them. They all had so much dirt on each other it made them have a kind of kinship, but each one was trying to bring the other one down.

Edgar was sick of the Kennedy's and he gave the order for him to be killed.

Like all Edgar's orders, these were carried out to the letter. Edgar had plants everywhere.

He knew better than to trust one man with such an awesome task. Oswald was stationed at the book depository and one of Marcello's stooges was on the grassy knoll, he fired the shot that killed Kennedy, not Oswald! Oswald knew the plan was to have someone on the knoll, and the two had only code names for one another. The poor sons– of–bitches were as dead as Kennedy when they accepted their offer. The man on the knoll got away because Oswald was getting all the attention, just as planned. The part of the plan the man on the grassy knoll didn't know, was the fate that awaited him, his life and death went unnoticed. No one directly involved could be allowed to live to tell the tale.

Oswald had always wanted to be a mob member so he did a little dirty work for the families, mostly Marcello. Marcello's operations were in New Orleans and Texas, and Oswald had lived in New Orleans and hooked up with Marcello there. Oswald was stupid and Edgar took advantage of his stupidity and his willingness to serve. Sometimes when we want something so bad, we become sloppy in trying to achieve it. That is why I have been so careful to plan all of this out for you. I don't want your quest for the truth to be sloppy. I want everything to fall into place when the time comes." "What happened to the man that killed Mr. Kennedy? Is he dead, too?" she asked.

"Well, another mob wanna be was Jack Ruby. Ruby was living in Texas. He owned a nightclub and thought he was a mobster. He liked the women and he liked feeling he had authority. He stayed in trouble all the time for petty things. He was another sloppy bastard that allowed his 'Johnson', wants and dreams to cloud his thinking. Edgar trusted him more than Oswald simply because he was more interested in having his name in the papers than anything else. He didn't want anyone else getting the credit for what he had done! Hell, he thought the country would give him some kind of award or something for killing the bastard the world thought killed Kennedy. He was sadly mistaken! Edgar could never let something like that happen. Edgar, having stooges in practically every police depart-ment in the country under his thumb, arranged for Ruby to get around Oswald as he was being transported to another place giving him press cre-dentials and permission to go in and out whenever and wherever he pleased. That's how he got right up to Oswald and pulled the trigger. The press was covering Oswald and Ruby was caught on film shooting him!

Unfortunately for Ruby, his demise had also been arranged, he was diagnosed with terminal cancer." She interrupted, "I thought cancer was a disease. I didn't know you could catch it!" she exclaimed with a scowl on her face.

"The United States had been delving into germ warfare. Deadly germs would be injected into the body, some forms were merely put on the skin like lotion and the skin would absorb it. Ruby was given a live cancer cell while he was in prison. The perfect murder! There was no way it could ever be traced! The only people who knew about it were the people closest to Edgar." "Were you involved with Hoover then, too?" she asked some-what confused by all he had said. "Yeah, I knew what was going on. I went to New Orleans the day before Kennedy came to Tampa. Edgar sent me there to make sure everything was going according to plan with the other families. Edgar and I had too much on each other for one to try to screw the other one. So instead, we were friends. The trust we had was born from fear. We respected that fear," he said. "I guess that's kind of like what mama told me about the snakes in the pit. She said they sensed when you were afraid of them and that caused them to be mean. She told me I would have to develop a respect for them and what they were capable of before I could ever handle them without them biting me. I never have really liked them, but I guess I respect them, out of fear like you said." He chuckled at her wise analogy, "I guess Edgar is a snake! He sure doesn't hesitate to strike if he is threatened! While I was in New Orleans, under-cover so to speak, Gus went with me. He was working for me to find out what Cal knew about Marcello. Cal never knew Gus was informing me about what was happening. Gus and I were always pretty close friends. Cal never knew." "You mean Uncle Gus was working against Uncle Cal! I can't believe he would do that! Did mama know?" "Your mama didn't care! She only cared about me. She learned it was too dangerous to know too much about her brothers or me. She just loved all three us unconditionally, what we did outside our relationships with her didn't matter. As for Gus and (he gritted and growled), Cal, it was Edgar's plan to have them pitted against one another, that way nobody suspected Gus was working for Edgar. Believe me, Edgar knew something about Gus that even his brother didn't know. Something that caused Gus to fear Edgar or he would not have worked against his brother. I never knew what he had on him, but it must have been something that would have put him under the jail!" She won-dered if Hoover knew! Maybe someone was punishing Gus for what he did to her!

He continued, "No one was ever the wiser about what really happened to Jack Ruby. Kennedy, Oswald, and Ruby all dead just as Edgar planned. He didn't want anyone around that didn't do as he said. Edgar is one bad bastard, Jacqueline. He gets what he wants and those who oppose his wishes do so at their own peril! You are the only one who will have this information when I die. You will need it someday. I told you, I have written a book called, *The Godfather*. I had a man named Puzo, Mario Puzo publish it under his name. It is based on my life and my family. He is not to ever tell where he got it. That will be up to you to do. He is to tell you and only you the truth about it when you ask. I left out chapters three and five; they belong to you. He was on his own with those two. Some of what I have just told you is in the chapters I withheld from Puzo. For the most part it is in code. Edgar would never have let me tell you or anyone else anything that would incriminate him. I'm not that stupid! I know my life would be snuffed out with no questions asked. I had to live long enough to tell you. The chapters I left out of the book are in Edgar's secret files. My deal with him was to give him information he wanted on my family, Trafficante, Marcello, and any other person or family that he could use. In return, he is to help you prove you are my daughter and give you the chapters when I am dead and you ask for them. I hope I can trust the son of a bitch; so far he has done what he said he would do. There are things I need to tell you about the book, the codes that are in the book, but it will have to wait until another day. This is an awful lot for you to understand and I apologize for slinging it at you so hard and fast, but I need to tell you, and this is the only way I can. I can't write this down it is too sensitive and it is what will give you your inheritance." With that he patted her on the head and motioned for her to come watch television with him. She found it hard to concentrate on Ice Hockey after hearing all that, but she tried.

The next day Lillian made pancakes for breakfast. Jackie thought she would be staying home, but she made an excuse to leave. "I'll be home in time to cook dinner," she said as she was putting on her coat. "There are plenty of sandwich fixings in the refrigerator. I know you two can manage." She patted Jackie on the shoulder and she was gone. "Where does she go everyday? She doesn't work does she?" Jackie asked. "No, she doesn't. She does a lot of church work when she can leave me. I guess she realizes we need the time alone and that helps her to get out, too. She has been good to me. Our relationship is friendly. I needed her to take care of me and she needed to take care of someone. Her husband died, Rob's father, and Rob married. She didn't feel needed anymore, I guess." "Do you love her?" "Um…I respect her, I care about her, I like her. I'm not in love with her. I'll never love anyone, but Irene, and I will be in love with her until I draw my last breath and beyond if it is possible!" He was looking directly into her eyes when he said it and she believed it. She wished he could tell her mother, but she knew he couldn't.

"I wanted to tell you more about the book. It is loosely based on me and my family. It has a great deal of symbolism in it. I changed the names and the places. The real setting for the book is Palmetto Beach and Tampa. You will recognize places in the book like the Twenty Second Street Causeway. The trial is the one Cal (girt and growl), and Gus were in that brought your mama back from California. The wedding was my sister's; I carried your mama to it. Do you remember meeting Walt Disney?" "Yeah, at the Sportman's Club. I was his hostess! He was really nice to me. I liked him." "Why didn't you take him up on his offer to send you to Paris?" "How did you know about that?" she asked bewildered. I sent word by Edgar, to ask Disney to do that for me. He and Edgar are pretty good friends." "I just thought he was being nice. I wish I had known he wasn't kidding. "Well, anyway, he is Woltz in the book. He was asked to put Frank Sinatra in one of his movies because Frank's career had taken a nose-dive. He told them he would if contract negotiations had not been completed. So, he didn't do as they asked, and one of his prize pony's head was cut off and put in his bed!" "Ooo…that's sickening!" she shrieked. "Yeah, it is, but it happened."

Many people will recognize themselves in the book. I tried to use names of real people, maybe spelled differently, or I would use a word or phrase that fit something about the real person. In the book I used the name Johnny Fontane for Frank Sinatra, but there is a sentence Johnny says that gives the real first name! I have codes and clues to who people are or were, and when you go public with all of this people will start finding themselves on the pages! Edgar has no idea you are being told these secrets, and he sure as hell doesn't know I wrote a book. When the time comes for you to make yourself known as my flesh and blood daughter, you'll need proof from me that you exist. On your birth certificate my name is listed as 'Glisson'. Glisson was my Irish family name. My father's family was from Ireland. He had nothing to do with the family business of my Mother's family. My grandfather, the 'godfather' used to call my father, 'the pet'. He allowed my mother to stay married to him because she was expecting me. He had one thing in his favor Irene didn't have; he was Irish Catholic. When my grandfather died, Uncle Guido took over. He tried to fill grandfather's shoes, but never did. He treated my mother and father with very little respect. When my father, Da I called him, became ill, Uncle Guido saw to it he stayed pretty much sedated and out of the way. My mother rarely left my father's side, which kept her out of the way, too. Not that she wanted to know about the business, she just wanted to be sure she had her standing in society and her money. Guido hated giving her money, he was a greedy bastard. The last summer my father lived he was doing fairly good, health wise. Mother had him seen by a specialist in Europe and whatever treatment he was doing helped. He even got to where he could play a little golf and swim. One morning he got up early for a swim and my mother went to get him for breakfast. He was floating face down in the pool, dead. Joe and I always believed Guido had him killed. He knew mother would not live long without him; she would grieve herself to death. She did. She didn't live six months after 'Da' passed away. If I could have found out for sure Guido killed Da, I would have killed him! He knew it, too. He was old and didn't live much longer himself.

I paid him back for everything he did to my parents and yours! While he was on his deathbed, I promised him I would carry on the 'Family'. I told him I would see to it the 'family' got everything it had coming to it. I did. Our family is now the most hated in history! The Patrillo family name is a disgrace all over the world; so don't ever use it! It is a good thing you were a girl! Otherwise, your life would be in danger until you died! Girls have no respect among families like mine. They are considered possessions, trophies. You will be alright," he promised. "Tell me about being a movie star," she pleaded. sensing it was not his favorite subject.

"When I first started my career in Hollywood my family wouldn't allow me to use either of my family names. At first, the studio billed me as Larry Fine. Then it was all screwed up and nobody knew who the hell I really was, so everybody just called me 'Curly'. There will probably be a mystery surrounding my 'real' name forever, but I was the most famous and everyone recognizes Curly! The name 'Curly' stuck, even Irene called me Curly! I was always recognized as the person I played on screen, which was good because nobody knew me for who or what I really was, except her! Irene saw through me and loved me anyway and that's all that mattered to me. She didn't care what my real name was, or what I looked like, she loved me for me!

Hollywood...that part of my life seems like a dream now. Many books have been written, lies told, I don't even want to know about it anymore. My only regret about being in show business is that you and your mother won't ever benefit from it. You will never be able to cash in on the Stooges thing; someone else is already doing that.

You'll benefit from my having lived, Jacqueline. Someday, you will be able to reveal the answers to secrets that have baffled the world for years! I intend to have the last laugh, you'll go beyond the laughter." Then he asked her to follow him into the bedroom. Once there he sat on the edge of the bed and motioned for her to sit in the chair. He reached into the drawer of his bedside table and retrieved an ink stamp pad, "I need you to let me take your fingerprints so that I can send them and some other information about you to Washington. When the time is right and you know the man in the White House, you'll be able to make your move." He took her hand and as if he had done this a million times before, pressed each finger in the ink and rolled it on a sheet of paper. As he did so he said, "When I finish, go wash your hands and come back in here. I need you to give me some more information." She did as he requested. "What is your social security number?" she told him. "When you get back to the states, you will need to change your name." He told her how and what name to change it to, (for safety reasons, Jackie will not reveal the name).

He had her describe every scar on her body. He began, "Show me the scars you got when the coffee pot fell on you." "You knew about that, too?" she asked astonished! "Jacqueline, there is very little about you I don't know. I have been watching when you didn't even know I was there. You shoot a good game of pool, by the way." He announced. "You're unbelievable! Why didn't you say anything if you were around. Didn't you think I wanted to see you, to know you?" "I knew, but I had to keep you safe. I couldn't take the chance. By the time my Uncle died it was too late. I had to leave the country. It just couldn't happen then. I'm just happy I have this time with you, to tell you what I need to tell you. God, I wish you were older so you could really understand all I'm telling you!

I'm sorry for all the times I wasn't there and all the times you didn't know when I was, I was there a lot and you just didn't know it. I came to the hospital when you were burned; I held you hand and kissed your forehead. I saw you in the Gasporilla Parade; sometimes when you were playing with Sally, I knew everything. I had a lot of people watching when I couldn't. I even signed my name in the Sky King plane as you did!" he said. "You were there when Uncle Joe took us to the park?" she ranted! He just smiled.

"Now, tell me about that scar," he said pointing, "A snake bit me! Not really a snake, but it was a reptile, in the pit. I used to work for Gus and Cal, (grit and growl from him) in the snake pit in the carnival. Did you know about that, too." she questioned. "Yep, I hated that for you and Irene. I wish you had found something else to do in the carnival besides taking your clothes off. I don't want you doing that anymore." his look of disappointment made her angry. "You know, if you had supported me, I wouldn't have had to take my clothes off in front of people! I could have stayed in school, learned to read and write and got a good job! You really shouldn't be so judgey!" she snapped. "I just want you to be a lady, like your mama. That's all I have ever wanted. That's why I wanted Walt to send you to Paris. Anyway, that's over and done with. I want you to get a book out of what I am telling you. Then you will have what you need. That's all I have left to give you. Now, what's your favorite color?" "Yellow", she answered. He continued with her favorite song, movie, food, anything he thought would be pertinent information in identifying her. Then he said he was tired and needed to rest. They would continue later. He lay back on his bed and took a nap. She went to her bed and cried about all the things he said, and how had she only known Mr. Disney was serious, her life and her mother's would have been different. She resented his disapproval of the things she had to do to survive, things she never would have done if she'd had a real father to take care of her.

Sensing her animosity the next morning, he decided to have a lighter type conversation. After breakfast he went into his room and called for her. She reluctantly answered his call. He closed the door revealing a full–length mirror, "Have you ever watched any of the Three Stooges shorts on television?" he asked. "Yeah, I've seen a couple of them. Never paid too much attention to them, though. Granny and Mama wouldn't let me watch them, because so many kids were getting hurt trying to punch each other's eyes out and bopping each other on the head! They probably just didn't want me to see you! You know, I don't ever remember seeing the Three Stooges after I saw you at the service station. I believe I would have recognized you after that. I know I would have, because I recognized you in that picture in the hallway, before I met you." she remarked. "Watch," he said as he curled his lip, "Can you do this?" she laughed. She tried a couple of times, and then he showed her again. They laughed when she finally got it. "Well, if they can't look at you when you do that and know who you belong to, they're blind!" he made her practice every day for the rest of her stay.

"There are still things you need to know, things I find hard to talk about, mainly because I don't want you to hate me for the things I've done or knew about and couldn't prevent. I know you're still full of piss and vinegar, and right now things that are important won't interest you, but I still need to tell you and all I can do is hope you will remember them when the time arises. I remember once when I held you on my lap and played patty cake with you." " I don't remember that", she said with regret in her voice. "Well, I also played another game with you. You would touch the buttons on my shirt as I said, rich man, poor man, beggar man, thief, doctor, lawyer, Indian chief. This is more than a child's game now, Jacqueline. You need to remember you are the rich man, poor man, and the beggar man. You will feel you are begging for what is yours, you've already been poor, and when you use the information I give you it will make you rich." Jackie winced as if she had just been given a spoonful of distasteful medicine. He recognized that he was giving her an awful lot of information and some of it was like a riddle, a puzzle. He realized she needed a day out. He had Lillian call Rob to take her into town the next day. He told her not to discuss anything he had told her. He also told her that people in town did not know him, as 'Curly' or any other name people in the United States would recognize. "Be sure you don't discuss me with anyone," he warned.

She made no remark, although she wanted to tell him that she had no intention of discussing him with anybody, he had nothing to fear there!

The next day Rob came to pick her up. She got the feeling he was a little irritated at being summoned again, he was respectful to him and followed his instructions to the letter.

The town was beautiful! Jackie had never seen so much snow! She was impressed with the beautiful buildings, her favorites being the quaint boutiques that housed the trendiest fashions. They ate lunch in a diner and the waiter who spoke both French and English fascinated Jackie.

When they returned from their outing Jackie told her Father all about the wonderful things she had seen. For the first time he was able to share in her life. He heard it from her, no private eyes, he was told about her day by her. He liked that; she wouldn't have admitted it, but she did too.

CHAPTER SEVENTEEN

The next few days they spent watching cartoons and sporting events. Jackie thought he was very smart where sports were concerned. He would explain every play and all the rules. She had to admit she would rather watch Bugs Bunny or Road Runner, but she thought he was funny when the team or person he was rooting for didn't do what he wanted! He told her about the mob being connected with some sporting events in the U.S. and how her Uncle used to scam at the dog track! As usual he would grit his teeth and growl at the mention of Cal's name. He still continued to tell her he would explain sometime. It finally dawned on her he was trying to keep her interest!

"Jacqueline, can you curtsy?" "Probably!" she answered indignantly. "But, why do I need to?" "Humor me, show me your curtsy.", he commanded. She curtsied her very best curtsy, "Well…" he said stroking his chin, "That's pretty good, but you need to go down just a little more and…" he took his cane and tapped her right foot, "Turn that out a little more." She did as he said. "Yeah, that's it. Go into my room and practice that in front of the mirror, you'll need to be able to do that when you meet the Queen." Jackie didn't question his motives; she knew he must have a reason for this strange request! She wondered when he thought she would meet the Queen, but a few months ago she would have thought she had as much chance meeting her father as she had meeting the Queen! So, maybe she would meet her!

That night at dinner Jackie found herself starring at her father as he pushed his peas onto his spoon with his knife. His hands were gnarled from a stroke he had suffered several years ago. She noticed the nicotine stains on his fingers and listened as he coughed so deeply his face turned red, nearly purple. She wondered if he would get through this one. "Are you all right?" she asked as he fumbled for his water glass. He swallowed and motioned for her to hold on with his twisted forefinger, finally he spoke, "You've been very sly with your smoking, Jacqueline, but you forgot I have known everything about you from day one. I hope you will look at me and see the results of a lifetime of smoking. I know I haven't done much for you until now, but I hope this will teach you a lesson and you'll quit while you're young." She could tell he wasn't feeling well so she made the excuse she had a headache and went off to bed, she lay for what seemed hours listening to his uncontrollable coughing spells and the ferocious sound of his breathing that echoed through the house. Lillian was his faithful servant. Jackie could hear her trying to get him to take a breathing treatment. He finally consented and the coughing stopped. His breathing wasn't as labored, but could still be heard. Somehow the sound of his unlabored breathing comforted her. She went to sleep.

The next day he seemed much better. He was in a talkative mood again. "I'm sure politics don't interest you much right now, but someday it will be important for you to understand some things about politics. You should be well informed about what goes on in your government.

I told you how J. Edgar Hoover had nearly every politician and many police department heads in his pocket. He taught his political puppets signals for voting preference. For instance, he folded his hands in the model of the children's rhyme, "Here's the church and here's the steeple, open the doors and there's all the people." he was doing the hand motions as he spoke. "If the politician was to vote 'yes' on a specific bill or to a question at a press conference, the steeple would be pointed up. If the answer was "no" it would be down." "Who gave the signal?" she asked interested. "Good question. Whoever Edgar appointed to call the shots at the meeting or whatever. There was always an assigned patsy for these things. It's important for you to remember this because someday the vote may be your business," he said. She was making the hand jesters with him trying to remember what he was saying. It seemed odd he would tell her these things, and yet she wanted to know what he had to say. Even now, however she had moments when she hated everything about him, because he could have done this, years ago had he really wanted to. She wasn't satisfied that he couldn't do any better; she just knew she couldn't dwell on it, not now. Now she had to savor the time she had with him, no matter what kind of secrets he had to share or what confessions he would make.

"I have a question for you, Jacqueline. There's only one mystery in all these years that I haven't been able to solve. Did your mother ever talk to you about someone kidnapping you when you were nine months old?" "Yeah, she said she rescued me all by herself. Why?" "That's when I had you taken," he said. "Did Mama know it was you?" "Yes, she knew, I was surprised she had enough grit to go after you! That's the mystery, how did she know which baby was you?" "My mole. She felt for the mole on the side of my face." he laughed, I knew it had to be something special! There were three babies in that crib that night!" "Who were the other two?" she questioned. "Babies, just babies," he answered vaguely. "There's something I want you to always remember, the second time you were kidnapped out of love!" he proclaimed. She hadn't really considered coming here with Rob a kidnapping, but apparently he did. He said, "There were five guys that could have brought you to me. They were told to let you choose, and you chose the one I trusted most. Rob is a good boy. I hope you'll find one as good as him someday. I'm sorry you developed strong feelings for him. That was a tough break. I have an idea that you'll find another guy pretty quick. Most teenagers do. That first love is the one you always remember, the one you never really get over. Was Rob your first?" he asked. "I've had a lot of boyfriends. I'm not too crushed; don't worry about it. Mama says we're survivors, I've lived through worse. I even saw a man killed once. I was with Uncle Cal, (he gritted and growled), Why do you do that!? She snapped. "Do what?" he teased. "You know what, grind your teeth and growl like a bear every time I say...his name." "Whose name?" he asked. "Cal". He gritted his teeth and growled again. They both started laughing. He got so tickled he began coughing again. A few minutes passed and he quieted down, "He saw to it I toted a few ass beatings. He hated me because I didn't buckle under to Trafficani and Marcello. He had an idea I was informing Hoover." "Were you?" "Hell yeah I was! When my family had my marriage to your mother annulled I wanted to destroy them as they had me. So I made a deal with Edgar to keep him abreast of all mob activities I could find out about. That's how he found out Kennedy was trying to stop the gun running and the plot Marcello and Trafficani had to kill Castro. Hoover wasn't pleased. He had been looking for a good excuse to have Kennedy killed. These things I am telling you because when you are older, and wiser, you will want to use the information to help solve the mysteries that will still exist. You will be a very important person, Jacqueline. You will have the power to solve a murder that will not be solved for many years to come. There will be many speculative reports about Kennedy's murder, but that is all it will be, speculation. Hoover is old and President Nixon wants him to resign. He won't, he'd kill himself and make it look like natural causes first! At Edgar's request I've spoken to Nixon to try and find out what his plans are for Edgar. Hell, Dick is wiretapping everything from the toilet paper to the phone. He can't prove it, but so is Edgar! I talked to Dick for nearly twenty minutes and Edgar made sure that part of his tape was missing. You don't get anything over on Edgar! He is crazy and fucking smart, he's dangerous! I don't know about Dick, but I do know Edgar has covered his paper trail. He put me here to live out my life, what's left of it; hell they think I'm already dead in Hollywood. They've had me dead since the late fifties or so! Edgar helped me keep you and Irene safe. I owe him for that. He advised me to send the information about you to the White House Counsel, he belongs to Edgar. The information will be kept under lock and key until you know the man in the White House, as I have already told you." "But, I don't know anybody that will be in the White House!" she retorted. "Sure you do. Just wait a few years. I promise you will know the man I am talking about. If all works according to plan and Hoover lives to retire he will see that you get the information. Do you know all the seven Dwarf's names?" he asked. "Doesn't everybody." "Yeah, you're right, but they will have a different meaning for you than anyone else."

For some reason she was feeling drained. She was tired and the riddled conversation caused her to feel like Alice in Wonderland, confused and lost. Perhaps as he said, she would understand all of this as time goes by. Now, what about the man you saw Cal shoot?" "Oh, it was nothing. He said he was just having fun." She remembered Cal had told her to keep quiet about that. I was little, it wasn't anything really." she yawned. He shrugged thinking she was just trying to shock him.

Lillian had made their favorite, hamburgers and fries. They watched a game of ice hockey and went to bed.

Day after day he revealed bits and pieces of her life. It amazed her that he knew all about the events that even she found trivial. "Whatever happened to Herman the Duck?" he asked seriously. Giggling she replied, "How did you know about him? Oh, yeah, you were there that Christmas Eve. I thought Mama had cooked him for Christmas dinner. We had a big old turkey that I didn't know we had, and I just knew she cooked Herman!" He laughed and laughed. "I didn't have Herman long after that, he flew the coup!" she said laughing.

"I want you to do something for me, Get that Bible over there and read some to me," he requested. Reluctantly she picked up the Bible, "Come closer, the light is better here," he said. She didn't have the vaguest idea why he thought the light was better. It was daylight and the whole room looked the same. Regardless, she followed his directions. "Read the Twenty–Third Psalm to me," he said. She fumbled through the book. Realizing she was having trouble, he gently took the book from her hands and turned to the chapter and verse. He spoke not a word as he handed it back to her. She began. Her stumbling over the simplest of words caused him shame. He knew it was because of him that her education had suffered. He helped her read it as a tutor would, saying every word she could not pronounce. She could feel her face turning red and when she looked at him, his face was red, too! She took her hands and gently with her finger-tips, stroked his face. " I guess you take after your old man more than you knew," he said. He took her hands in his and kissed them. She smiled, as she retrieved her hands, "I knew I must look like my father, Mama is more like Granny. I think they had Indian in them. Granny used to say she and Mama got their high cheekbones from the Indians. So, I know there was Indian in Granny's family," she said. "Cherokee, I think I remember your Granny saying. She was wise. I liked her, she was a good woman and it saddened me when she died. I couldn't come to her funeral, but I sent your mother flowers. Did…"She interrupted, "Red roses! I remember that! They were so pretty and I remember Mama smiled when she got them. I remember because I was so worried that Mama would never be all right again after Granny died, all she did was cry. But, when she saw those roses and read the card, she smiled, and I knew that with time she would be alright." she spoke with such happiness. He was smiling as she spoke then he said, "I'm so glad. Your Mama was and still is, the most beautiful and wonderful woman I have ever known! Damn I miss her! Come on; let's go watch Bugs awhile.

Jackie noticed that when Lillian was around, he didn't talk much. She wondered about their relationship, even though both had explained it to her already, she was still curious.

She could tell he respected Lillian. He never raised his voice or cursed in front of her, or made any rude remarks. He thanked her every time she did even the least little thing for him. Jackie resented she never had the opportunity to see him treat her Mama so well, she wondered if Lillian had any tattoos! "Did you Tattoo Lillian like you did Mama? Lillian looked astonished. "That will be all for now, Lillian," he said as if speaking to the hired help. "Jacqueline, some things about my relationship with your Mother are private. I do not wish to discuss my business with you or about your mother with Lillian. Please don't remark about anything in my past around her," he said sternly. "Oh, I get it, you don't want to mix your awful past with your wonderful present! That's fine with me! Does she even know you had a life before all this?" she said as she motioned sarcastically at his meager surroundings.

"You don't have to be so insolent, Jacqueline. I just want what I tell you to be yours. Someday you will understand that I am giving you a gold mine. If you will just settle down and soak it all in so that you will remember what you need to when the time is right.' "Why don't you just write it down and give it to me?" she queried "Most of it has been written down for you. I have told you it's under lock and key, in code, and someday you will have to present some of the things I tell you in order to be allowed access to the papers." "What happens if the 'cancel' or whatever you said changes or dies. Like Nixon, what if he isn't President when I need the papers. I don't understand."

"Do you know Nixon, Jacqueline? Have you ever met him?" "No." "Well, then, you don't know the man in the White House. The papers are in a locked brief case. It's sealed with a government seal. I am being protected by the government because I helped Hoover out, as I've already told you, my name is not the same, it's now Tom Goings (this name has been changed for the purpose of this book). When I die you will need to know this. There is a gravesite in California where they claim I was buried around the late fifties. I wasn't as you can see!" he laughed. "I left Hollywood because my family needed me and the studio didn't renew our contract. Hell, we left one afternoon and the next morning they wouldn't let us back on the lot. Show business is worse than the 'mob', at least when the 'mob' gets tired of you or they had used you all up, they killed you and got you out of your misery! Hollywood shows no mercy! Both are dangerous, you should stay away from both!" Granny made me promise her that I would never go to California. She said it was going to fall off into the ocean!" "I told you I liked her, she was a wise woman. Hollywood swallowed up a lot of people. It didn't treat your Mama good when she was there," he said. He recounted a story about a Hollywood party that he and Irene had been to. He told her that a rape, sexual orgies and drug use was filmed on the end of an existing film, the *Miracle on Thirty Fourth Street*.

The last thing I did before leaving Hollywood for good was getting a friend of mine to help me sneak onto the lot and put a secret message on that reel. Nobody knows about it, except Edgar. He wanted the original reel so he could use what was on it to blackmail some of the people on it. I gave it to him. When he dies it will be found if he doesn't destroy it, so when you start releasing information as proof of what I am telling you, that will be one of your aces in the hole. The rape will be painful for you. So when you see it don't hate me. There were too many famous and prominent people involved in it for me to do anything about it. There was too much drinking and dope going on, nobody realized what they were doing including me!" he admitted. He recounted as much of the story as he could remember or as he wanted her to know. "Who got raped? Was it Ma…" He interrupted, "Don't say it! Don't!" he changed the subject quickly and just in time. Lillian walked in.

Jackie wanted him to answer her almost asked question, but she knew he never would. She never mentioned it to him again.

The next day Lillian was there until late afternoon. She cooked dinner and put it on the table. 'I'll be back in the morning. My sister is sick and needs me to stay with her tonight. Jacqueline, you'll be kind enough to help your father if he needs you." she put her coat on, bid them a good evening, and left.

Hardly a word was spoken at the table. When they finished eating and she was washing the dishes, he said, "If you and I could do anything in the world together, what would you want to do?" She drew a deep breath, gathered up soap suds in her cupped hands, and blew them into the air, then said, I would want us to take a hot air balloon ride." "Really? Why that?" he asked surprised. She sighed, "I'd like to be high above the ground and look down on all the buildings and trees, and stuff. I've climbed all the way up the double Farris wheel, did you know that?" "I'm afraid I missed that one!" he said smiling, "But, I did hear about it!", he wrinkled his eyebrows as he spoke.

"Well, at first I was really afraid, but then when I got to the top and looked all around I felt…I don't know, free and powerful! It was a natural high. You know? Anyway I've been up that high and I'd like to see what it's like higher up," she said dreamily. "You could do that in an airplane", he noted. "It's not the same! You couldn't feel the air on your face, and the breathlessness you experience the further you go up. An airplane has walls, it's not the same," she said shaking her head. She was surprised when she realized he was writing down what she said. She didn't question him, she knew he was doing it to put with 'her papers' as he called them. "Tell me a story about something that happened to you when you were young. Something that hurt, but gave you strength and power. Something that you could now look back on and laugh, but wasn't funny then." Again she took a deep breath, wrinkled her nose, bit her lip, dried her hands, and sat down to think. "Uhm…well, Oh! Several days on the way home from school these twins." he interrupted "Boys?" "No girls! And they were mean! They kept pulling my hair and stuff. It was awful! I finally told mama why I came home crying every day. She dried my eyes and kissed me on the head, then said, 'Jackie, if you come home crying tomorrow, and you haven't stopped those brats in their tracks, I'm gonna wear your bottom out!' She said she didn't want me starting anything with them, but she expected me to stop them if they started anything! I was shocked at mama, and I knew she wasn't playing. So the next afternoon I made sure I left school first and when they came up to me I turned around real fast and bopped both of then upside the head with my tin Mickey Mouse lunch box! I got them both with one swing! They never bothered me again! Mama was waiting for me on the front porch, she saw me coming and knew I wasn't crying. I saw her break the switch over her knee and throw it in the yard as she ran to hug me." he smiled as he took down her words. "What do you want that stuff for? How will that be important?" she asked. "Someday that story might help you prove who you are. I'll tell the story and nobody but the two of us will know you told me. See?" "Yeah, makes sense to me."

Afterwards they watched television awhile and then he said, "I hate to ask you to wait on me, but if you could get me a glass of water and help me with my medications I would appreciate it." She did as he asked. When he had finished, she lifted his legs around onto the bed and covered him up. "I've never tucked anyone in before," she remarked. Then she patted him on the head, "Goodnight."

Curly lay awake and thought how ironic it was that his daughter was tucking him in. It should have been the other way around all those many years ago. Tears rolled down his cheeks as he thought about how it should have been with him and Irene and Jackie. A family, a Norman Rockwell picture kind of family! Damn his 'family' damn them!

Jackie was having her own thoughts about how things should be. She reminisced about the one time she was barely awake when he tucked her in. How she had savored that time on many nights after Gus slithered out of her room. Damn her father! Damn his family!

CHAPTER EIGHTEEN

Lillian was back the next morning before Jackie awoke, breakfast was waiting for her. "Rob will be by after breakfast to take you to town," her Pop said. "Lillian has a friend that owns a boutique called the La Cher Cheq. She thinks you are kin to Lillian somehow, just let her think what she wants. Don't go into why you are here, it's none of her business. Anyway, one of her regular salesgirls is out and she asked if you might be interested in working in her place a couple of days a week while you are here. I know you're probably getting bored being around an old sick man all the time, young people need to be out and about more." "What would I be doing?" she asked interested. "I'm not sure, and it's up to you. You don't even have to go see about it if you'd rather not." "Oh, I'll see about it. It might be fun!" she got dressed and as she was waiting for Rob she put her black leather jacket on to take Champaign out, her father gritted his teeth and growled as he did at the mention of Cal's name. She laughed, "Now, what are you gritting your teeth about?" she asked with a smile. "That hoodlum jacket!" he replied. "What do you mean by that?" "I'd just rather see you in something more feminine." She held her hand out rubbing her thumb over the tips of her fingers in jest of 'give me the money." He remarked, "You're fixing to be working, then you can loan me some!" they laughed. Rob came in as she went to take Champaign out. A few minutes later she returned, they left for town, "You and your old man seem to be getting along well." "Yeah, I guess. You know, I want to like him. I just can't stop thinking about all the time he wasted. We could have been a real family, you know?" "I know, but that is in the past and you can't go back. You just have to decide if you want what he has to offer now. If you do, you have to go forward. If you don't, go home and worry about the past that can't be brought back. Someday all of this will be the past, and if you throw it away are you any better than he is?" That sounded wise to her, something to think about at least. She leaned her head back to enjoy the scenery.

The boutique was quaint; Jackie just fell in love with the clothes, the atmosphere, even the owner, Elyse Pierre. She was a colorful lady, dressed to the nines in her store fashions and drenched in Channel. She carried a white teacup French poodle named Babette in the palm of her hand all the time! Babette was cute with her fake diamond collar, but she had the most annoying little bark!

Elyse was taken with Jackie's waist length hair. She would have her put it on top of her head, pull it back into a French twist, and when she could tear herself away from Babette, she would French braid it and put gem-stone clasps in it. Jackie could choose any outfit in the store, put it on, and walk around twirling and flittering throughout the shop modeling the outfit for the customers. Elyse told her she was making business boom! At the end of the day, whatever she had modeled was hers to take home. She was also paid a weekly wage, under the table of course, as Jackie did not have a green card.

Curly was happy having her there with him. He never mentioned her leaving, he knew she would let him know when she was ready to go.

At Christmas she received a new blue ski jacket to replace her 'hood-lum' jacket. Christmas was not really celebrated because of Lillian's religious beliefs. He honored her wishes. Jackie wasn't really disappointed that Christmas wasn't celebrated. She never really cared for it much anyway. She could only remember one Christmas when she got what she really wanted. She knew now he had been the one to grant all of her wishes that year, and nothing could have topped that Christmas anyway, so the lack of decorations and tinsel didn't matter. She loved the coat and her new clothes she had gotten at the boutique. They were spring fashions, how-ever and it made her miss the warmth of home. She knew when she left she would never see her father again. She wasn't ready to let go of him, but at the same time she still harbored ill feelings for the time he wasted and for some of the hurt he had caused her mother. "Why were you so mean to Mama?", she asked again. "Mean? I don't think I was 'mean' to her. I loved her. I tried to protect her," he excused. "Well, why did she cry all the time? Every time I heard her and Granny talk about you, it either made her cry or she had to leave." she whined. "I know it's hard for you to understand, Jacqueline. I've tried to explain things to you as best I can. If you want to ask me anything, I'll try to answer your questions. I really don't know what more to say. I just know how it was, and I couldn't do one damn thing to change it." "Is there more explanation in that book you wrote?" "Not really. A lot of the book was how I wish it had been. I think the other information will help you understand why I had to do the things I did. The information you are entitled to will be your legacy, your inheritance. You will have what you are entitled to if you are careful and wait until the time is right before you show your hand. You will have the two chapters I left out of the '*Godfather*', the reel of with the studio party and identification of politicians, movie stars, directors, producers, judges, that witnessed what was happening and didn't do one damn thing, but turn their backs and pretend they were deaf and blind. You will have a list of people and their functions, what they did and whom they did it to. This information will make you a very powerful person in the United States!

It is in code so you will need to remember what I have told you. Don't be discouraged if you don't remember it right now, or if it doesn't make sense to you now. It will, all in good time. Pay attention to what goes on in the government and all around you when you get home. I know your lacking in formal education, but you are not stupid and you will be able to retrieve from your memory what you need, when you need it.

If nothing else, Jacqueline use what I have told you, find someone you can trust to tell your story to and let them write a book for you like I did. I hate to repeat myself, but I do it so you will remember it!

The information is yours and you will be placed in a room with a fireplace to go through the papers. Burn it, don't burn it, it will be up to you what to do with it. Your inheritance will be the book you get from the secrets I tell you! So make wise decisions when given the opportunity."

They spent much of their remaining time together playing cards, (he taught her to play poker as he had her mother), watching cartoons, ice hockey, and roller derby, and eating as many hamburgers as they could talk Lillian into making! He enjoyed watching Jackie and Champaign romp in the snow, he sat by the window and occasionally she would make a snow ball and throw it at him. Once she made a snowman outside his bedroom window and put her leather jacket on it and a lighted cigarette in its mouth! He laughed when she held up a sign that read, "Hoodlum Tom!" then he cried, as did she.

"What ever happened to Uncle Joe? We stopped seeing him when we went into the carnival." "Well, it's hard to say. He would have been the next in line to run the 'family', when I left. There was no other real family to do it. I told him he would be in a great deal of danger if he hung around. I don't know if he did or not. Some say he died in a car accident. His car was found in the Bay. Some say he left the south. I really don't know. Besides Irene and you, I miss him and Gus and that's it! I hope he got out alright. I would hate to think I signed his death warrant!" "I hope he is all right. I liked him," she said sadly.

A few days before Jackie was to leave was the only time he had left the house since her arrival. He didn't have visitors except for his physician, who came weekly, and Rob when he was asked to come. Jackie knew this must be important if he was getting out. Lillian drove. They didn't go far before entering a cemetery and stopping. Curly broke the silence by laughing and saying, "I've lived a long time since I was supposedly dead and buried in California! This is where I will be buried, Jacqueline. This may not be my final resting place, however, because there may come a time when you will need to have my body exhumed for proof of who I am, or was, and who you are. If you do, I would like to go back to the United States, home. Lillian will be buried by her husband, so she won't miss me!" She smiled. I would like to be buried near your mother if that is possible." Noticing the look on her face, he continued, "Don't get me wrong, I hope she lives forever! But, if you could find it in your heart to find a place for me and a plot beside me for her, it would mean a great deal to me," he said softly. She made no comment, mostly, because she didn't know what to say, but partially because she didn't want him to have too much peace of mind. She still harbored some resentment. She hoped one day she could let go of it, but she couldn't yet.

He broke the silence again, "Lillian hasn't said anything about this to anyone, and I hope she won't get upset with me for sharing it with you now. I would appreciate it if it went no further than this car." Jackie shook her head. "Lillian isn't well either. She is suffering from breast cancer that has spread to the lymph nodes." Jackie gasped, "Lillian, I'm so sorry!" Lillian smiled and nodded in gratitude. He continued, "You'll be on your own when the time comes. Do not write the name of this place down any-where. You should be able to remember it by this, (he sang a little tune for her that she could remember, that had the name of the cemetery in it). This will be another ace in the hole for you. You'll be able to find this place when you need to, trust me." He tapped Lillian on the shoulder as if he were giving the order to leave. They drove back in silence.

The last few days of their time together was spent in review of what she had been told and shown. She curled her lip, curtsied as if for the queen, named the seven dwarfs, showed him the signs for the political voting, sang the ditty for remembering the cemetery, and recounted some of the information she was given. He was happy in all that she remembered. "I am very proud of you, Jacqueline. You have listened and learned well! You will be fine. Just continue to watch and listen, not letting anyone stand in your way of what is rightfully yours," he leaned in closer to her and whis-pered, "This is what I mean when I tell you to go beyond the laughter. The laughter is the part of my life that has been dead for many years, now. Your inheritance will be from the information about my life beyond the star years. I am glad we had this time together. I know you are still young and angry with me in ways. I can only hope as you mature you will be able to forgive "me," he had tears in his eyes as he hugged her. She didn't hug him back, but she didn't pull away either. She wanted to do both!

Leaving was harder than she ever imagined it would be. She knew she was leaving behind the man she had always wanted to know, hug, kill at times, and love. She had developed a different aspect of her thoughts regarding this man named, 'Curly', the man she had known only as 'him' for such a long time, but now wanted to be renamed 'Pop'. She thought of all the times she wished he were there so she could call him anything at all. Now it was she who would be walking out of his life, and somehow the mere name one wanted to be called seemed very unimportant. Her life would never be same, and she knew his wouldn't be either.

He was in his room when she was ready to leave. Lillian told her he was waiting for her in his room. When she got to the door he was standing, looking out the window with his back to her. It was spring now and he had the window up. The birds were singing and everything seemed right with the world. "You all packed?" "Yeah, I think so," she answered. "I can't give you the address because it's too dangerous for me and you as well. I have arranged for your flight back to Tampa. Rob will stay with you awhile to keep up the façade. I know I don't have the right to ask anything of you, Jacqueline, but will you tell Irene I'm sorry and that I still love her? Don't discuss anything I've told you, she knows most of it, what she doesn't know she doesn't need to know. I don't want her hurt anymore. I know I've told you a great many unbelievable things this last year, don't worry if you can't remember everything I've said. Events will happen to trigger your memory, and then there is the briefcase that contains all you will need to prove you're my daughter. I'm proud that I have been fortunate in keeping your mother and my relationship private. People will learn from you what you want them to know." He was silent for a minute; she could tell he was sniffling. "I'm glad I came. Now when I think about you I'll think about more than you standing against that car! I'll think about you wearing tan and green pajamas fighting with the officials during a hockey game!" she said half laughing trying to lighten the mood. He laughed, coughed and continued, "I've always loved you. and I always will, no matter how many miles are between us," he proclaimed. I will still know everything you do until the minute I draw my last breath. I have loved you always and I will love you forever!"

She walked over to the window, he turned around and they embraced for the first and last time. I love you, Jacqueline," he whispered. She had finally heard the words said the way she had dreamed he would say them to her! The words she had waited her whole life to hear. He tightened his arms around her. She wanted to tell him she loved him, she whispered, "I…have to go, Pop. Take care of yourself." she broke his grip and ran from the room, the house! Through tears she waved goodbye to Lillian and mouthed, "take care of him. Thanks."

As the cab made it's way down the long, pine tree lined drive, Jackie noticed a covey of birds, and she continued crying as she thought about her relationship with her Pop, and how it reminded her of a baby bird being pushed from it's nest to survive on it's own, never to see it's parent again.

She had mixed feelings for him now. She couldn't really say she hated him anymore; hate was too strong a word. Perhaps she understood him more than she ever thought she would. She wanted to love him, but it was hard to admit she did or ever would. She couldn't understand how her mother could have continued to love him after all she went through, but she had come to realize that he didn't actually do anything to her, but he didn't do anything to make her life any easier, either. Nor did he do anything to make Jackie's life better. She wondered if she would ever really understand her parent's relationship, and yet perhaps she didn't have the right to understand it. After all, who was she to judge others for their feelings and motives? She wondered if her mother knew what she was really doing in Canada. She had phoned her in town several times since she had been there, and she never once questioned her about what she was doing or when she was coming home. She had to keep pretending to be with Rob, and she hated to have to deceive her mother. She hoped she would understand if she ever found out the truth! Maybe she wouldn't question her motives, she never seemed to question her father, she just let him do whatever and lived for the time he would be with her again.

She thought about all the times her Pop had said he saw her and her mother when she was growing up, that she knew nothing about. She wondered just how much her mother really knew about him. Somehow she just couldn't believe that she knew nothing about him. How could two people in love with each other so much, never have a real ending to their relationship? She fell asleep and when she awoke it was time to buckle her safety belt to land.

CHAPTER NINETEEN

Irene had been traveling with Cal and Gus running the Torture Rama. She got tired of being on the road and her diabetes was working on her health. She decided to move back to Tampa about a month before Jackie came home. Mikey's house was empty and he was glad Irene wanted it back.

Rob had the taxi take them directly to Irene's. It didn't occur to Jackie that she didn't even know her mother was not with the carnival. It would be several days before it would dawn on her that this was the way her father had always done, and that's how her mother remained unaware that things were even happening to her! Everything was so methodically planned and fell into place so well it appeared natural. She realized he really did know everything that went on. Even now he was aware that Irene was back in Tampa. She smiled as she realized he really had known all that went on in their lives from the beginning!

When the taxi stopped, Jackie jumped out and ran up the front steps. Irene heard the taxi horn just as Jackie reached the front door; Irene opened it. "Mama!" Jackie said as she threw her arms around her, "I've missed you so much!" "I'm glad you are home,"

Irene replied, "Let's get your things unpacked." They went into Jackie's room. "So, you finally met your father!" "How did you know?" "Jackie, I've known your father nearly all my life! I know how he operates! The day you left someone slipped a note under the door telling me you were fine and would be home when you decided you wanted to leave. It was signed with the same signature your father used; I knew it was him. What did you think of him?" "I don't know, Mama. I can't talk about it, not now. Oh, he said to tell you he was sorry and that he still loved you and always would." Irene blushed and asked no more questions. Jackie never told her the things her father asked her not to.

Gus and Cal retired from carnival life as well. Gus was working on a legitimate shrimp boat, Cal's health was failing and he and Billy were both on government money. Jackie never told either what she learned from her father.

Rob stayed about three weeks. Jackie had met the boy next door, Tony. They began to talk and flirt some and as Curly had directed, "When Jacqueline finds interest in another boy,

Rob and you are satisfied she will be alright, you can leave." Jackie would never see Rob again. It was a little hard when he left, but she had someone else to concentrate on.

She would think of her Pop, Lillian, and Rob often, probably more often than she wanted or that she would admit.

About a year and a half after Jackie returned from Canada she received a small package wrapped in brown paper, hand delivered by Mikey Michaels. There was no note, no signature, just one dingy lace glove wrapped in a tear stained handkerchief with a monogrammed 'C'. She knew he was gone. Mikey had no idea where the package came from or what it contained. Her name was scrawled across the brown paper in childlike writing. She wasn't sure it was her father's doing, but it was a nice thought. When she got home she pressed the handkerchief to her lips and placed it gently in her dresser drawer. She never told her mother about receiving the glove. She decided when her Mother died she would place it in her coffin. She hoped it would be a long, long time.

It was nineteen eighty–one before Jackie knew the man in the White House. Just as her Pop had told her, there were events that triggered her memory. She tried to contact President Ronald Reagan regarding the briefcase that was being held in trust for her. She received no response from him or his staff. Instead, and investigation and arrest of well known mob bosses ensued. Some of the material her father had told her was in the briefcase was used to convict these men. Information that only her father had and now the White House was using!

Hoover had died the summer of the year Jackie returned from Canada. Therefore, he could be of no help to her. His secretary had shredded many of Hoover's private and confidential papers, Jackie's were probably among them.

The remainder of the contents of the briefcase was passed down from Counsel to Counsel ending with Vince Foster, White House Council to President William 'Bill' Clinton. Jackie is convinced that Hillary Clinton is responsible for the briefcase and it's contents ending up in the hands of Hollywood's greedy movie moguls, as well as, the higher echelon of the Disney Corporation. Jackie saw Mrs. Clinton on national television stating she had sold the papers she had found to Hollywood Studios.

Details connected with Jackie's conversations with her father began showing up in top rated movies such as, *War Games* where the main characters use, 'Rich man, Poor man, beggar man, thief...etc.', to break the computer code to the White House. Then a made for television movie, *To My Daughter With Love,* had a great deal of similarities such as the hot air balloon and the name Jackie appearing in it.

Even in the recent *Wag the Dog,* similarities were countless!

The picture of Irene with her breast in the wringer washing_machine appeared in *Hustler Magazine* in the early eighties.

Jackie feels her information was stolen, she feels she was cheated out of what was rightfully hers. The part of her father that had been recorded just for her to do with as she saw fit was never acknowledged by anyone she tried to contact for help. She realizes her writing skills may have played a part in that, however, she knew she was to be known by her signature. She, like her father trusted the information would be hers when the time came. Thus far they were wrong.

Now, all she has left are the memories, the truths her father told her and the will to do as he said on several occasions, "At least get a book out of the secrets I tell you. That will be your legacy."

Now she understands what he meant when he said, "You'll go beyond the laughter."

What Happened To...

Irene–after retiring from carnival life, resided in Tampa, Florida
    where she was continually harassed by authorities regarding
    knowledge of Curly's whereabouts or demise.
    She died several years after Curly of complications related
    to diabetes. Her family believes she was murdered, even
    though her death was listed otherwise. She was taken to the
    hospital for a toe injury that would not heal because of her
    diabetic condition. She was operated on for breast cancer
    for which she had never been diagnosed. She was only forty–
    seven years old. Jackie buried the glove and handkerchief
    with her mother.

Curly–died of cancer in nineteen seventy–five, not the late
    fifties or early sixties. He was not in California when
    he died, nor was he buried in California. Jackie still
    remembers the limerick he taught her revealing his true
    burial place. She plans to exhume his body sometime in the
    future and bury him next to her mother as he requested.
Gus–died of lung cancer at the age of seventy–five. His
    perversion was never revealed until now.
Cal–like his sister, had diabetes. He was a double amputee.
    He died of kidney failure at the age of fifty–six.
Billy–died of a heart attack shortly after Cal.

Joe Allums–presumed dead.
Mikey Michaels–owned the Saratoga until his death. He died of old age.
Cracker Boy–Last known address, Raiford Prison.
Rob–whereabouts unknown
Lillian–died of cancer. Jackie does not know if she died

before or after her father.

Champaign–died of old age.

Jackie–is married and has a dog, a bird, and an aquarium. She has
Spent many years attempting to retrieve the papers her
father left her. She realizes she could be harmed by telling the truths her
father revealed. She remains somewhat out of the public eye. She refuses to
give her real name, the names of her family members, her father's assumed
name, and any other pertinent information she feels will
enable her to prove to the world she is Curly's daughter.
She has no doubt as to who she really is or who her father
was, nor can she admit her true feelings for him.

ABOUT THE AUTHOR

Grace Garland has been a public school teacher for twenty years. She began writing at an early age and had a weekly news column for several years. She lives in the South with her college freshman daughter and her "little son" Nikki, a white bischon friese. Writing is her passion and she tries to communicate this passion to her middle school students. When not teaching or writing, she spends time with her parents in Florida.

0-595-20846-0

Printed in the United States
1317600002B/96